Auditioning for Film and Television

Auditioning for Film and Television

Secrets from a Casting Director

NANCY BISHOP

Bloomsbury Methuen Drama
An imprint of Bloomsbury Publishing Plc

B L O O M S B U R Y
LONDON · NEW DELHI · NEW YORK · SYDNEY

Bloomsbury Methuen Drama

An imprint of Bloomsbury Publishing Plc

Imprint previously known as Methuen Drama

50 Bedford Square	1385 Broadway
London	New York
WC1B 3DP	NY 10018
UK	USA

www.bloomsbury.com

BLOOMSBURY, METHUEN DRAMA and the Diana logo are trademarks of Bloomsbury Publishing Plc

First published in Great Britain as *Secrets from the Casting Couch* by Methuen Drama in 2009

Reissued with a new title, additional material and a new cover design by Bloomsbury Methuen Drama in 2015

Crossing Lines © Tandem Productions GmbH and TF1 Production SAS. All rights reserved.

Sniper Reloaded © 2011 Sony Pictures Worldwide Acquisitions Inc. All Rights Reserved. Courtesy of Sony Pictures Worldwide Acquisitions Inc.

Nancy Bishop has asserted her right under the Copyright, Designs and Patents Act, 1988, to be identified as author of this work.

British Library Cataloguing-in-Publication Data

A catalogue record for this book is available from the British Library.

ISBN: PB: 978-1-4725-2636-6
         ePDF: 978-1-4725-2417-1
         ePub: 978-1-4725-2628-1

Library of Congress Cataloging-in-Publication Data

Bishop, Nancy, 1966–
[Secrets from the casting couch]
Auditioning for film and television : secrets from a casting director / by Nancy Bishop. — New edition.
pages cm
ISBN 978-1-4725-2636-6 (pbk.)
1. Motion pictures—Casting. 2. Acting–Auditions. I. Title.
PN1995.9.C34B57 2015
791.4302'8—dc23
2014037311

Typeset by RefineCatch Limited, Bungay, Suffolk, UK
Printed and bound in India

This book is dedicated to Joel Kirby, my teaching partner and loving colleague, who helped me develop the technique that we teach in our master classes.

Permissions

360, written by Peter Morgan, directed by Fernando Meirelles, BBC Films.

Anne Frank: The Whole Story, written by Kirk Ellis, directed by Robert Dornhelm, ABC Productions.

Before Sunset, written by Richard Linklater, Kim Krizan, Julie Delpy, Ethan Hawke, directed by Richard Linklater, Warner Independent Pictures.

Child 44, written by Richard Price, Tom Rob Smith, directed by Thomas Espinosa, Scott Free Productions.

Crossing Lines, created by Edward Allen Bernaro, Tandem Communications, Bernero Productions.

Hitler: The Rise of Evil, written by John Pielmeier, directed by Christian Duguay, CBS Productions.

Mirrors, written by Alexandre Aja, Gregory Levasseur, directed by Alexandre Aja, 20th Century Fox.

Missing, created by Gregory Poirier, ABC Productions.

November Man, written by Michael Finch, Karl Gajdusek, directed by Roger Donaldson, Relativity Media and Irish DreamTime.

Rectify, created by Ray McKinnon, Sundance Channel.

Sniper Reloaded, written by John Fasano, Robert Helford, directed by Claudio Fäh, Sony Pictures.

'This is a terrific guide for young actors travelling though the tortuous, torturous event they call "an audition". I read it cover to cover and then went out and bought copies for all my kids because, truthfully, it puts an experienced eye on pretty much all of life's early encounters.'

Donald Sutherland

'You only get one first impression when you walk in that room. Are you ready? Nancy Bishop will guide you so that not only will they take the moment to see you, but more importantly, they'll see what you can do. Nancy's wealth of experience will give you an understanding of what doesn't necessarily have to be a nerve-wracking experience but rather one that through being prepared can be uplifting and a chance for you to shine. Do yourself a favor, don't read it just once.'

William Fichtner

'Nancy Bishop provides a clear, concise approach to casting and show business for the professional actor. It is an invaluable resource with current, up-to-date information on what Casting Directors, Directors and Producers are looking for in a variety of audition situations as well as useful information on how to market oneself in the international casting arena. You can trust Nancy to give you the straight answer to the challenging questions of how the audition process works, whether you are in Prague, London or Los Angeles and anywhere in between.'

Donna Morong, Casting Director and Owner, Aquila Morong Studio for Actors

'Nancy's book is a fascinating read for career-minded actors. It's a no-miss read . . .'

Aksel Hennie, Actor

'Nancy Bishop has put together not only an incredibly helpful book for actors but for all in the entertainment business. Bishop's writing is clear and concise in touching on such issues as the process from auditioning and what one can "expect" when dealing with casting directors. Nancy is part of the International Casting Network and speaks a number of languages which is always helpful.'

Avy Kaufman, CSA, Casting Director of *Lincoln* and *Life of Pi*

Contents

Preface

Nancy and I worked together on *Hannibal Rising* and since then we have continued our collaboration, giving workshops and seminars exploring the art of casting. I therefore feel uniquely qualified to recommend Nancy's book both as a film director and an occasional lecturer.

We shared a unique experience while teaching in Kiev, Ukraine, shortly after the events at Maidan Square in 2014. Our charge was to consult around one hundred Ukrainian TV executives about the casting process and we had prepared a two-day lecture complete with PowerPoint presentation, illustrated with copious film clips.

After an hour of general and introductory remarks we took a quick coffee break. A large and rather brusque executive called us into the backroom and verbally roughed us up in a style somewhat reminiscent of the Soviet era demanding that we teach 'the science of casting'. Nancy and I caught each other's eyes during this dressing down – '*the* **science** *of casting*'? We laughed about it later over a fine dinner of Varenyky and horseradish vodka; casting is hardly an exact science, though you might say that choosing the right actor is a type of chemistry.

Inasmuch as there is no science to auditioning, there is a sort of method that can be analysed and learnt. Nancy has managed to break down the process in an organized way that is extremely helpful to actors, as well as other industry professionals. *Auditioning for Film and Television* addresses all of the important themes and details including strategies, marketing, how to prepare, and unique perspectives from (as she says) 'the other side of the looking glass'. We directors, after all, can be just as nervous as the actors about our work. It is very helpful for actors to keep this in mind.

I rely on casting directors to put good actors in front of me. If I have faith in my casting director, when I meet an artist for a role, I already know they're good. I'm not necessarily looking for the best actor but rather the actor with whom I can work best. So I think that Nancy's advice is well taken to think about auditions not as 'tests' but simply as meetings with respected colleagues. I book actors who can take notes and help me discover the story: actors who will be a pleasure to work with in circumstances that are often fraught because of tight schedules and all the day-to-day problems that occur on a shoot: actors who are brave and inventive, but who turn up well prepared and will deliver when you are losing light and only have one take left: actors who are there for the team and not just for themselves.

Enjoy these pages. It's a good book for an actor to keep on the shelf as a reference – a type of actor's bible, as it were.

Peter Webber

Acknowledgements

Special thanks to:

This book would not be possible without the help of my many supportive colleagues.

I gratefully thank my manager and friend Derek Power of Kahn Power Pictures, and my assistant David Stejskal. To my agent and friend, Jeremy Conway. To Anila Gajevic, for supporting my work in the Balkans.

To Tariq Hager and Tomas Krasauskas and all of my colleagues and students at the Prague Film School.

Megan McConnell at CSA has been available and supportive, as have my casting director colleagues: Lana Veenker, Amy Jo Bermen, Debbie McWilliams, Beatrice Kruger, Meg Liberman, Suzanne Smith, Meagan Lewis, Michael Sanford, Mark Hirschfeld, Donna Morong, Deb Green, Nina Gold, Harika Ujgur, Pound Mooney Casting, Lori Wyman, Luci Lennox, Bonnie Gillepsie and Avy Kaufman.

To all of my many interns from NYU, Zach Brunswick, Jasmine Cho, Nelly Simonian, Jennifer Leevan, Jeremy Davidson, Caitlin Kirby, Darby Weyland, Kirsten Hutton and Clayton Buchanan.

To Gary Marsh and his staff at Breakdown Services and Chris Gantos at Castit for their access to information.

To Michael John and the Actors Centre in London. Paul Michael's 'The Network' in NYC.

To the actors who shared information, Lara Rossi, Karel Roden, James Babson, Dufflyn Lammers, Sarah Marie Brown, Brian Colin Foley, Cengiz Dervis, Miraj Grbic, J.D. Evermore and Alexandra Callas.

Thanks to my cherub, Anna Rust, who helped me on the social media research and will be too busy working as an actor to help me in the future, I'm sure.

Lastly, thanks to photogapher, Barbara Sitar.

Introduction

This book came to life from the synthesis of my love for teaching and my experience as a casting director. I have directed thousands of actors over the years in audition sessions, but the casting process does not allow the time and energy to give actors the concrete feedback they need to forward their careers. In this book, I hope to bridge that gap

Why a new edition?

The original title of this book was *Secrets from the Casting Couch: On Camera Strategies from a Casting Director*. In this updated version, I believe the new title more accurately reflects the contents of the book. This is a comprehensive guide for three kinds of actors:

1 beginning actors who wish to learn success strategies for the casting process;

2 experienced actors making the transition from theatre into film;

3 experienced actors who want to increase their chances for landing the role.

In *Auditioning for Film and Television: Secrets from a Casting Director*, I offer concrete strategies for auditioning in the casting room, and for marketing and advancing a career in the Internet age.

What's new in this book?

In the marketing section readers will find new chapters on:

- internet marketing;
- social media;
- how to effectively use IMDb;
- living and working in the world market.

Since trends have evolved, there are revised chapters on the following:

- self-taped auditioning;
- headshot presentation;
- show reel or video clip presentation.

Regarding practical exercises, there are updated chapters with:

- new scene analysis;
- revised exercises;
- new sight reading monologues.

Video section

I have also collected some concrete examples of good auditions, both self-taped and in the casting room, from actors who have booked roles. This can be viewed at www.vimeo.com/116852346, using the password '61sh0p'.

Acting is not just an art, it's a craft

It's a myth that some actors have 'it' and other actors don't in front of a camera. While it's true that some people are naturally more 'watchable' on screen, there are skills that actors can learn to develop and improve screen presence. When you first learned to drive a car, you didn't just head into rush hour traffic. You had to learn and practise. Screen acting and auditioning require the same type of training and commitment.

This book addresses auditioning in the Internet age. Since publishing the first edition of this book, the phenomenon of the 'self-tape' has become even more prevalent. Entire films are cast now by casting directors selectively presenting clips that actors have created themselves. A few years ago, for example, I cast a film called *Sniper Reloaded*. International financing dictated that we cast actors in Europe and the USA, but the filming was in South Africa. Operating in a tight time frame and budget, we had no time to fly actors and casting directors around the world to meet the director personally. I requested that actors tape themselves, short-listed the talent and the director interviewed actors on Skype. Actors must be prepared and in possession of the technical knowledge and tools to tape themselves and get the audition to the casting director in a timely fashion. Samuli Edelman is one actor whom I cast in a lead role in *Mission Impossible IV: Ghost Protocol*. Brad Bird selected him from a self-cast that Samuli taped at his summer home in Malta, while his wife operated the camera and read off-screen. Thousands of actors have now booked roles in this way. Chris Hemsworth earned his role in *Rush* through a self-taped audition that his agent sent Ron Howard.

The good news is that casting is not just about luck. Nature didn't dole out 'good auditioning' genes in the DNA of certain actors and not in others. Auditioning, like acting itself, is not just an art – it is a craft. A craft can be learned, practised and perfected. There is no mystery to it. *Auditioning for Film and Television* teaches practical techniques for improving your audition method.

I come from a theatre background, and fell into casting by accident. I learned about film acting by directing castings for supporting talent on over nearly one hundred major studio and network projects to date. Through the years I have broken down casting into a system of techniques and strategies, which I teach at casting workshops internationally. In these pages you will learn this system. Good auditioning cannot be learned solely from a book, however: you have to practise, practise, and keep practising.

I will not pretend to offer a formula for success because there is none. I can offer strategies, but for each 'rule', there will be an exception. For example, I would generally say that an actor should prepare well for a casting, but it's a crazy business. There will be times when an actor will prepare like mad, then another actor, without having read the text, will book the role instead. Showbiz ain't fair.

The 'secret' in the book's title is that there is no secret. To excel you need to work hard, and never stop studying the craft. Auditioning means competing in an ultra-competitive arena. It's not for the faint of heart. It is, in fact, for the terminally insane. But if you've decided that you're crazy enough to join the carnival, then welcome to this book.

PART ONE

Audition success strategies

Twelve strategies

Actors who work are actors who . . .

1 Enjoy auditioning

2 Prepare

3 Make choices

4 Determine the stakes

5 Tell the story

6 Act and react in the moment

7 Play in the eyes

8 Possess an inner monologue

9 Commit to the scene

10 Stake a claim on the role, take a risk

11 Listen

12 Make their own work

1

Enjoy auditioning

Nothing was ever achieved without enthusiasm.

RALPH WALDO EMERSON, Philosopher

Enjoy the casting process

Actors who get cast are actors who *enjoy the casting process*.

When I was casting *Dune* for the Science Fiction Channel, I met one talented actor, Anna Rust, who was auditioning for the role of Alia. We called her back to read with us a few times. In the end, we decided that she was a little too young for the role (she was only four at the time). When I told her father that unfortunately we had not chosen Anna, he said, 'It doesn't matter. She thinks she already did the film'. In a sense Anna was right. She did play the role. For those few minutes when she came in for her initial meetings, she was playing Alia in front of camera, for an audience of three; myself, my assistant and the camera operator. We then showed it to the producer and the director. The casting was a film in itself. She played Alia in a mini-film.

Anna did eventually book roles as a child actor, and she is now a young woman and still working as a professional today. Her story drives home the importance of attitude. There are plenty of things that an actor doesn't have control over in the casting process. One thing that actors always have control of is attitude. Having a persistent, positive and professional approach is at least 50 per cent of the game.

Anna succeeded for two reasons, both having to do with attitude. First, because she enjoyed the process, and, second, because she approached the casting as if she already had the role.

The old adage in theatre is that if the performer is enjoying himself, so will the audience. The same goes in an audition. Enjoy it, and we will too. If auditioning is an excruciating experience for an actor, you can guarantee that it's a painful experience for the casting director as well. No one wants to work with an actor who is miserable and down on themselves. Yet some actors approach the audition as if it were an execution. If you come to the audition, as if to your death, then we may put you out of your misery ('Thank you. Next!'). On the other hand, if you're enjoying the process, then we may ask for more.

Auditioning is an intrinsic part of the actor's life. There are a few superstars in the world that don't have to test, but even top actors still have to read for roles. Daniel Craig had to read for *Bond*. Marlon Brando famously had to screen test for *The Godfather*. Even Pierce Brosnan admitted to me that although he doesn't have to 'read' any more, he is still obliged to meet with producers and their spouses, which he perceives as a kind of audition.

If you dislike auditioning, then you're going to dislike being an actor. Find a way to make friends with this process. Talented actors get turned down at castings all the time. Why? Because there's only one role and many actors. Each time an actor reads for a role, however, she is building a relationship with directors that can eventually lead to a booking. Here's a lesson from Thomas Watson, founder of IBM, and one of the most successful men in the world: 'If you want to increase your success rate, double your failure rate.' Jack Nicholson had to audition five times to get into Lee Strasberg's acting studio in New York, and Harvey Keitel a whopping eleven times. Jon Hamm had to audition eight times before the team at AMC was convinced he could play America's favourite rake, Don Draper in *Mad Men*.

Certainly, it's not easy putting yourself on the line again and again. An actor going to meetings day after day without any success can easily begin to doubt her skills. Thoughts like this begin to take over: 'I never get roles. This director doesn't like me. I messed up my last audition. I've already been to six castings this week and no one wants me.' These attitudes are killers that infect performance, and poison effectiveness.

Think about the things you're good at. If you're a good cook, the chances are that you like cooking. If you're an excellent skier, you probably love skiing. It works the other way too. If you love skiing, then you're likely to become a good skier. If you like auditioning, you're probably good at it. Remember casting commandment number one: *Enjoy the process.*

Transform your nerves into enthusiasm

The entertainer's journey through fear is the burden and the blessing of performance: it's what invests the enterprise with bravery, even a kind of nobility.

JONATHAN LAIR, *The New Yorker*

When you are nervous, it means that you care and that you're invested in the outcome. Nerves are not only a positive sign, they are a condition of success. It's the dizzying sense of fear that can either launch your audition to the next level, or capsize you into distress. If you're nervous, then make nerves your ally. Nervousness is energy. Transform your anxiety into enthusiasm. To be enthusiastic originally meant to be possessed by a god, or inspired by a celestial source. Enthusiasm is that inner energy that fuels our love for our art. Bring it with you, and create a divine performance.

Enthusiasm does not mean you have to kiss up to the auditors or fetch the director's slippers. Approach the professionals that you meet at the audition as respected peers, not superiors. An over-willingness to please and be 'liked' by your auditors can fuel the kind of negative nerves that will swamp your performance. Successful actors are not desperate for the job. You're not there to prove anything. We already know you're an actor. That's why you've been invited to the casting. Read for the role the way a star does – as if you already have the part. Claim the casting, the space and time it takes to do your work, then gracefully exit.

Bring your personality with you

Sometimes actors leave their personality behind when they come in the door. I've witnessed many actors, who normally possess a well-developed sense of humour, entering with a stone face. Why? Personality is so important to our profession. Remember that it's a job interview as well as a reading. No one wants to work with an actor who has no sense of humour or personality. You don't have to concentrate on being charming, just on being yourself. 'You're doing an autobiography every time,' said Dustin Hoffman. How can you do an autobiography if you've forgotten yourself?

Personality is what gets an actor the role. I don't mean that people with fun-loving personalities get cast and those who are grumpy don't. Often directors are looking for a quality, an essence, a part of that actor's chemistry that fits with the role. They may be seeking, for example, a lightness, a heaviness, a world-weariness, a bounciness, that *je ne sais quoi* that makes us individuals. The great acting teacher Michael Chekhov called it 'individual atmosphere'. There's an alchemy to casting that's beyond the thespian's reach. While actors like to think that they are perfect for every role, director Stephen Frears described the director's 'opposite philosophical position'. We're interested in 'what your quality is – there's nothing you can do about it'.

When I was casting Ridley Scott's *Child 44*, Agnieszka Grochowska told me that she had no energy for the audition. She was exhausted and cranky from taking care of her newborn baby who was keeping her up all night. She auditioned anyway and this frazzled quality is precisely what director Daniel Espinosa liked and what got her the role of a mourning mother who was begging for justice after the death of her son.

At a certain point in the casting process, there will be at least a handful of actors who can play any given role. From that short list, the performer who books it\ is the one who projects the quality that fits with the director's vision of the character. John Wayne spoke of film acting as 'pushing your personality through'. Celebrated film director Bernardo Bertolucci says that each face has a secret, a mystery, and through his work he seeks to unlock the mystery in the faces he casts. It's personality and individual atmosphere that interest casting directors. Even imperfections can get an actor the role. The late Peter Postlethwaite made a living from a scarred, pockmarked face. Sometimes it is the thing we are the most insecure about, the imperfections that distinguish us from the rest.

Bare yourself

The act of performance always involves vulnerability. Look to the ancient roots of theatre. In ancient Greece, theatre was a religious rite, a ritual. The performance was a sacrificial act in which the actors went forth in front of the community to experience the pain and pathos of tragedy. Thespians acted out the horrors – the deaths, the bloody fratricides, the betrayals – in place of ordinary citizens, to purge the audience of these atrocities. Performance is terrifying because it involves baring oneself. A psychological survey revealed that speaking in public is what people fear the most, even more than death. Yet performers do this every day. Performing takes great courage because it demands the actor's vulnerability. Be courageous enough to expose yourself in the casting process, warts and all.

When I was working with Peter Greenaway, he would say to each actor who auditioned for the role of Eisenstein (*Eisenstein in Guanajuato*) 'I need your heart, your soul, your mind and your prick' (always emphasizing the word *prick*). While in this case he meant it literally (there was full frontal nudity), there is a degree of emotional nudity in any acting job. The actors who learn to stretch out of their comfort zones are the most succesful.

> According to most studies, people's number one fear is public speaking. Number two is death. Death is number two. Does that sound right? This means to the average person, if you go to a funeral, you're better off in the casket than doing the eulogy.
>
> JERRY SEINFELD

Things to remember from this chapter

- Enjoy the audition.
- Transform your nerves into enthusiasm.
- Make friends with the process.
- Approach the audition as if you're already playing the role.
- Bring your personality with you.
- Allow yourself to be vulnerable.
- Interact with the casting director as a respected peer.

2

Prepare

Actors who get cast are actors who prepare.

An *Actor Prepares* is the title of Constantine Stanislavski's first book. This early twentieth-century Russian director revolutionized acting by introducing a system to naturalistically approach character. Stanislavski's basic orientation is just as germane today as it was one hundred years ago. The Stanislavski questions fit perfectly into an approach to screen auditioning. When you are given a side (a section of the script), what is the first thing you do? Do you just highlight and memorize your lines? You need to scan the text for information that will help you play the role, concentrating on key facts that will fuel your choices in a short amount of time. Stanislavski stresses establishing the *facts* of the scene by asking the 'w'-questions:

- Who am I?
- Where am I?
- Who am I talking to?
- What do I want?
- Where are the changes?
- What are the stakes?
- What page are we on?

> In transmitting the facts and plot of a play the action involuntarily transmits its inner content.
>
> *Creating a Role*, CONSTANTINE STANISLAVSKI

No one can act in a vacuum. It is amazing to me how many actors come into an interview without having done this very basic homework. This is Acting 101, and when I teach this in my audition technique classes, actors roll their eyes, thinking that I am telling them something basic that they already know. Even very experienced professionals sometimes neglect to determine these basic choices and end up swimming in a sea of too many possibilities.

How do you get the answers if you can't read the entire script? The first thing you should ask is, 'Can I get a copy of the script?' It's true that productions are getting more and more protective with scripts, but you will never know unless you ask. It will likely involve signing an NDA (non-disclosure agreement). Woody Allen doesn't even give out the title of his films during the casting process. Luci Lenox, who cast *Vicky Cristina Barcelona* in Spain, issued paper sides at the audition itself and no one was allowed to take them away. If this is the case, you may be surprised by how much you can learn by reading just one scene in a script. Most of the information you need will be embedded in the scene. Hopefully your agent will also provide a brief synopsis of the plot, prepared by the casting director. (See Part Seven, to find examples of scene analysis.) Certainly the scene will provide at least basic answers to these questions. Work with what you know; that's all you need and that's all any of the actors have, so you're on an even playing field. If you really feel like you can't answer these questions, you can most certainly ask the casting director when you're reading. I respect actors who ask questions. It reflects a thoughtful and professional approach.

Who am I?

> Who's there?
>
> First line of *Hamlet*, by WILLIAM SHAKESPEARE

Identity. This is the first question in drama. The answer could be simple. I am an American teenager travelling through Europe. I am a Madame of a bordello. I am a scientist. While it's important to answer the question, it's equally important not to over-analyse. This is an instance when Stanislavski's method, or its misinterpretation, is over-wrought at an audition. I've seen actors prepare a long list of questions about a character: what is the character's favourite colour?, what does she eat for breakfast?, etc. For a casting call, stick to the basics. Time is limited. Don't go into too much detail about the character or you obfuscate your objectives. The actor doesn't need to do a Freudian analysis of her character's relationship with her mother for each audition.

Research

Find out as much as possible about the project. Information is power. Is it a historical drama? If the project documents a real period, then this character might have actually lived. There's so much information you can get on the Internet, that there's no excuse not to do your research. When we were casting *Charles II* for the BBC, almost every character was someone who had lived. Even when you're just reading for a crowd member shouting 'Death to Catholics!' know the context for that period of history. In *Hitler: The Rise of Evil* for CBS, there were actors who came in to read the role of Rudolf Hess, without knowing who this historic figure was. They had a harder time acting the role. James Babson, who did the research on Hitler's deputy, got the part.

Where am I?

See the location, and play it. Certainly the side will provide the location. Are you inside (INT.) or outside (EXT.)? Are you in a public or a private space? The way we relate to our spouses at the kitchen table is different from how we would relate to them in a crowded train station. If there are other people around, maybe you don't want them to hear your conversation. When an actor hasn't answered this question, it shows. They look like they are floating in space. This might be appropriate if it's a movie about astronauts.

'Playing the space' is an important concept. For example, I had to audition actors for a scene in *Hellboy* that took place in an underground tunnel. The actors had to imagine that it was dark and wet, and they had to really see the monsters that were coming to swallow them up. The actors who were cast were the ones who could see the space and make it real. In the world of CGI (computer generated images), it's increasingly frequent to experience this on set too. You won't be provided with the dark tunnel and with the monster – all you'll have is a blue screen to play off of. Samuel L. Jackson said of his work on *Star Wars*, 'They put you in a big blue room and say "Fight 'em." So you put your little kid hat on and fight 'em.'

Who am I talking to?

What is your relationship to the other character? Is it your mother? Your lover? Your enemy? Do you like this person? Do you know this person? Your character needs or wants something from the other. This need drives the scene. For example, 'I want this person to love me.'

Here is a monologue from ABC's *Anne Frank, the Whole Story*, written by Kirk Ellis, and directed by Robert Dornhelm. Edith Frank (played in the series by Tatjana Blacher), is hiding from the Nazis, cooped up in an attic with her family and another family during World War II.

```
244 INT. ANNEX - OTTO/EDITH'S ROOM
Edith and Miep sit on the edge of Edith's
bed . . .


                    EDITH
               (after a beat)
          You hear how they all talk. 'After
          the war.' I say nothing. What can I
          say to them? Mrs. Van Pels - you know
          how she carries on. Who is she to
          criticize? The things she says about
          the children. The children, Miep.
          Anne. Margot. Otto says we must be
          hopeful. Hopeful for what?
```

```
                    MIEP
You mustn't think such things, Mrs.
Frank.


                    EDITH
I know. I have to be strong. But for
how much longer? If only this waiting
would end. At least then I could be
certain. Miep - we're not going to
make it. No - it will have a bad end,
I'm sure of it now. It doesn't matter
for me. But the children, Miep.
What's to become of the children?
```

Who is Edith talking to? She's talking to Miep (Lili Taylor), someone who lives outside of the cloistered attic. When I ask my students to figure out what she wants from Miep, they usually make the choice that Edith needs Miep to be her mother now. She needs Miep to do what she's doing all day with her daughters. Edith needs Miep to say, 'You will survive. You're going to make it.' In other words, she desperately needs and wants Miep to disagree with her when she says, 'we're not going to make it.'

What do I want?

This is the most important question. The character wants something and that's why we're interested. One of the first Greek tragedies ever written was about Oedipus the King. His objective was to lift the plague that was killing his people in Thebes. In Shakespeare's *Henry V*, Henry wants something. He wants to conquer France, and marry Catherine. All of his actions in the play derive from this objective. Storytelling has not changed much since Greek times. Your character, like Oedipus, like Henry, must want something. There is no acting without objective. As obvious as this might sound, actors often come into auditions without thinking about what the character wants.

Devise an active verb to spring your character into action. To act means to perform an action. That is why actors are so called. This is where many actors fail in a casting. They have gone to acting school and learned about objectives, yet they don't make vital and crucial enough choices. The best action verbs are the ones that take a direct object. For example, think of the name of the other character. John. I want to vanquish John, I want to change John, I want to hug John, or I want John to hug me. If you choose a verb that takes an indirect object, it weakens the scene. For example, I want to complain to John. I want to find something out from John. Do you see how those objectives are not as strong, precise and direct? They give you less to play.

Some actors forget to choose an objective because they're so obsessed with their own objective, which is to get the role. So they think their objective is to impress the director. This is not your objective! Choose your character's objective and then the scene will work, and your objective will likewise be achieved.

Another trick is to look at the page number. It will be on the upper right corner of the script. Be careful not to confuse it with the scene number. Usually a script has about 120 pages. So if you're on page 10, you know that you are at the beginning of the film. That tells you that it's an introductory scene. This is the first time we're meeting the character.

Or is it the last scene of a horror movie? That tells us that we've already encountered this monster many times. Looking at the page number gives you an idea of scale and tone. Are we at the end, at the moment of climax, or are the characters first being introduced? Remember that you are a storyteller, so it's important to know where you are in the story.

Where are the changes?

The camera loves change. Change and contrast are built into a good script, and exist in most any scene. Often a change occurs when an actor discovers something. Some actors make their discoveries before they come on. It is always more interesting to see a change on screen rather than off screen. Mark where the change happens. How does it change the scene and the objective? Where does it change? What does the character learn? For example, regard this scene in Richard Price's script, *Child 44*, based on the popular novel by Tom

Rob Smith. Tom Hardy plays Leo Demidov, a ruthless KGB agent digging for information about an enemy of the state, named Brodsky. Zina (played by Ursina Lardi) is an innocent neighbour, and possibly the suspect's lover.

```
(Page 11 of the script)

21 INT. APT. OF ZINA GUBINOVA

Another woman reduced to cowering in her own
home. Leo eyeing her.

                    ZINA
           He was a good neighbour.

                    LEO
           A good neighbour?

                    ZINA
           I meant . . . he was considerate with
           the noise. He was polite. That's all.

                    LEO
           How come you are the only one in this
           building saying that?

                    ZINA
           Because I'm telling the truth. That's
           why. He was lonely, I'm a widow. We
           used to play cards - He was a good
           man.

                    LEO
           A good man?

He takes out his notepad, writes this down. A
GOOD MAN.
He underlines GOOD. Studies her eye movements.
He puts the notepad down.

           So you have no idea where Anatoly
           Brodsky is. You're just saying he was
           a good man?
```

                    ZINA
        There's no betrayal in saying that.

                    LEO
        You sure? Before he was a good
        neighbour and now he is, a good man.
        So you've changed your testimony all
        of a sudden?

                    ZINA
        You're twisting my words, sir.

                    LEO
        So now you're in charge? Making judgements.

                    ZINA:
        No.

                    LEO
        I want to know what YOU know. That is
        the game here.

Leo notices her hands are shaking.

        Would you like a cigarette?

Zina nods. Leo hands her a cigarette, lights
it. Lights one for himself, too.

                    ZINA
        The tobacco doesn't fall out of these
        ones-

She tries to smile. Leo just looks at her.

        They taste good too.

                    LEO

        I know. So . . . your good friend,
        Anatoly, might actually be a good
        man. What about your sister? She knew
        him too?

ZINA

What, what has my sister to do
with this?

LEO

Well, nothing – or everything. It
depends. Unlike you, your sister has
children of her own, right?

Zina looks at him, nods. Stares into the
ground. Leo can see her fear growing like a
cancer. Leo stubs out his cigarette.

LEO

It's odd . . . how close they have
become to you. You're like their
mother, right?

ZINA

Why are you saying that?

LEO

What you don't want is to be put on a
train going far away from here and
never being able to see those kids
again – because of what? You
protected a traitor.

Zina holds her breath. Fights with the tears
pumping out of her eyes. Leo pauses. Looks
around. Zina is trembling now. Leo takes out
his pad again. Leo detaches the page from his
pad; dangles it – A GOOD MAN.

LEO

This is all I have to report from
you. What else? You helped him too?

ZINA

No, no – Sometimes I would post his
mail for him. That's all.

```
                        LEO
          That's all? You're helping a traitor?
          Mail to where . . .?


                        ZINA
          Kimov mostly, to an old colleague
          from the medical corps.


                        LEO
          Name?

She looks pleadingly at Leo; if she gives him
the name, she's killing
the man.

          Name?


                        ZINA
          Okun, Semyon Okun.


Leo crumples her death ticket. Shamed by her
desperation to survive, Zina covers her eyes.
```

Tom Hardy's character drives the scene and controls the beats, while Zina discovers each tragic moment.

Zina begins the scene by defending her neighbour and sometimes lover, blind to the cruelties of the Stalinist regime that punished many innocent Soviet citizens. She proceeds as if her honest testimony will exonerate him.

Where are the changes?

The first change is marked when she discovers that Leo Demidov will vilify her neighbour no matter what she says.

'You're twisting my words, Sir.'

A second discovery comes decisively on the line:

'What, what has my sister to do with this?'

Here she realizes that if she does not betray her neighbour, both she and her family will be convicted as well.

The cigarette marks another change, a break in the tension. Props can be another natural moment to make a change.

The final crushing discovery comes on the last line when she realizes she has just killed her lover, having no choice but to reveal the name of his contact in Kimov.

'Okun, Semyon Okun.'

Her objective changes from exonerating Brodsky to saving herself. Her stakes are life and death.

Things to remember from this chapter

Establish the facts of the scene by asking the 'W'-questions.

- Who am I?
- Where am I?
- Who am I talking to?
- What do I want?
- Where does the scene change?

3

Make choices

Actors who get cast are actors who make choices.

Make an actable choice that is clear to you and easy to play. Keep it simple. Actors tend to make complicated choices that are difficult to play. For example, 'I think I love her, but I'm not sure.' A more decisive and playable choice would be: 'I love her and I want to shag her brains out on the kitchen table right now.' This objective is specific and there is a strong image that guides it. Turn your choice into an action verb. Do not choose negative objectives because they are not active and harder to play. 'I don't want to talk to him', is a weak choice because it doesn't give you anything to play. In fact, it gives you a reason to leave, but you need a reason to stay in the scene. A more active and therefore easier to play choice can become, 'I want to punish him.'

'I want to leave' is a particularly weak choice because then you would just leave. It's more interesting to explore what is keeping you from leaving. In Stanislavski's terms that is called the obstacle. Is it because you still love him? If we have a crush on someone but don't tell them, then what is keeping us from telling them? What's at stake? What do we have to lose if we tell them? Rejection? Manhood? Self-esteem? Pride?

An actor I know once told me, 'When a man and a woman get married, the husband wants his wife to stay the same and she always changes. The wife, on the other hand, wants her husband to change, and he always stays the same.' Take the wife's perspective when making your choices. Will the other character to change. Prove to him that you're right and he's wrong. Drama involves a competition between two characters.

What are the stakes?

When I was a young woman living in Chicago I took a self-defence course, where I learned an ancient parable. 'A wolf chased a rabbit. The wolf was running for its meal. The rabbit ran for his life. The rabbit lived.' The rabbit had more at stake than the wolf. In your audition, be the rabbit, not the wolf. Make the choices where the character has the most to lose, the most at stake.

A strong choice is easier to play. At a casting workshop, an actor was performing a blank scene (see Part Six) and he had not bothered to make any choices about why he was on stage, what his motivation was, what he was playing. He had decided who he was and where he was (on a couch with his girlfriend) but had not decided what he wanted. So the performance was flat and lifeless. I asked him to do the scene again but to decide what he wanted. The second time the scene was equally dead. I asked what he had chosen and he said, 'I wanted her to go get ice cream.' Unless he was hypoglycemic and at risk of dying from lack of sugar, this was a very uninspired choice, as well as being inactive and difficult to play. Think about stakes. What is at stake for the character? What has he got to lose? What will happen if she doesn't get the ice cream? In his scenario, not much. In the hypoglycemic scenario, then his life was a stake.

Films are often about sex and violence. Contrary to popular belief, this is nothing new. Sex and violence on screen (or on stage) have existed for all of recorded history, evidenced in ancient Roman theatre, the blood and gore of the Jacobean stage, as well as today's slasher movies. Therefore choices involving sex ('I want to get her into bed') and violence ('I want to kill him') are often appropriate. Even in more subtle genres, the characters' motives can almost always be reduced to these most basic terms – a fight for power, survival, love or money. Go for the strongest choices possible and they will drive your performance.

The objective is simply the action of the scene. Stanislavski tells us that an objective should have attraction for the actor, making him 'wish to carry it out'. Keep the objective simple and clear. The objective has to be something that makes sense in the circumstances of the film. Your choices should be robust, but not random. Serve the writer, the story, and the facts of the scene.

The audition differs from work on set because it is an opportunity to make diverse choices. Once you have the role, you are expected to repeat the scene the same way, more or less, each time. On set, the director usually establishes a master shot, and then she will shoot it from different angles and in close up. To play it differently each time will disrupt the flow and continuity of the scene.

When auditioning, however, I would recommend the opposite. Make at least two different choices for the scene before you come in. If you get multiple takes, try it a different way each time. Experiment with the script as you would in a rehearsal. The casting director might say, 'Ok, try it again a different way.' She might not suggest an idea. This may be because you're the 59th person in that day, and she's exhausted, or it could be because she wants you to be the brilliant one. You're the artist, so come in with ideas. She might also direct you to play the scene in a certain way and then you have to adapt to her directions even if they are completely opposite from what you prepared.

Here is an example of a scene from CBS's *Hitler: The Rise of Evil*, written by John Pielmeier.

```
Sc. 405D INT. OBERSALZBURGH HOUSE - GELI'S
SHRINE - DAY

Angela unlocks and opens the door to Geli's
room. Eva steps inside, looks around,
frightened a bit, but also fascinated. She
reaches for a brush on the dresser, but Angela
warns her:


                    ANGELA
          Don't touch. He'll know you've been
          here.
                (Eva pulls her hand away. Another
                     beat of silence.)


                    ANGELA
          You can't compete. You're alive and
          she's a memory. His memory. Not mine.
          Not the real Geli.
```

```
            (fighting tears)
I can't bring her back and I can't
change what I allowed to happen, but
I can warn you, Fraulein. If you show
any fire, any will of your own, he'll
turn you into this. This is his
ideal. Not you. Never you.
```

Here Hitler's sister enters the room of her dead daughter, Geli. The 16-year-old girl has committed suicide because of Hitler's obsessive control. She is speaking to Eva Braun, Hitler's mistress. If the actor gets three chances to play the scene, what are some different choices she can make?

1   To warn Eva. The subtext would be, 'Get out of this relationship soon or Adolf will kill you, like he did Geli.' This is motivated by concern.

2   To threaten Eva. The subtext: 'Get the hell out of my daughter's room, or I'll kill you.' This is motivated by anger.

3   To scare Eva. Subtext: 'We will all end up like Geli, but there's nothing we can do.' This choice would be motivated by helplessness.

Contrasting choices

Judith Weston, in her book *Directing Actors*, advises, 'Whenever you're not sure what to do with a line, find an opposite. If a scene isn't working, do it wrong.' Although her advice is to directors, it is equally useful to actors. Don't make the obvious choice. Make a contrasting choice. Looking for the humour is a good tactic. Find the humour in sad or scary scenes. A sudden nervous giggle in a scene when you're scared out of your wits can be very effective. Conversely, find the pain in a funny scene. Comedy is almost always at someone's expense, and involves deep pain. Your eyes might betray something different than your words. The words, 'I'm leaving' might mean I love you. The words 'I love you' might mean I'm leaving you. Find the contrasts. Any scene that is about love is also about hate, and vice versa.

As in life, we often don't reveal what we mean. In fact, we rarely do. Make sure that you're making the right kinds of choices. Decide what objective to play. Be sure to avoid the pitfall of choosing to play an emotion or a character over an objective.

An actor who gets cast plays objectives not emotions, adjectives or character. Objectives come first. Caution! Here are the mistakes I see:

Mistake #1. Playing a character before an objective

Don't judge the character. If you come in thinking, 'This character is nasty, I'm going to play a nasty guy', then you're putting character first. The character doesn't think he's nasty, he's just acting in his own interest. He wants something. Sometimes misguided directors give this type of direction too. 'Play him nastier.' When you hear a direction like that, translate it into actor's language – an action verb. 'I want revenge', for example.

In an interview, Robin Wright Penn was asked about her role of Claire Underwood in the hit Netflix series, *House of Cards*, in which she plays the Lady Macbeth-esque wife of a Senator. 'What is it like to play such an evil character?' the interviewer asked. 'She's not evil, she's just motivated,' she answered. In her mind every action is justified. She has to like the character and identify with her.

In CBS's *Hitler: The Rise of Evil*, Hitler didn't think he was evil, he thought he was saving Germany from what he saw as impurity. Robert Carlyle had to approach the role not as a bad guy but as a living, breathing person who had goals. He played someone who wanted a pure and glorious Germany. He left it to the audience to judge the character.

Another pitfall is when the script judges the character. One time an actor did a very strange read, and then she asked me, 'Should I play it more naïvely?' When I looked at the script, I noticed that the screenwriter had decided to describe this character as naïve, which was not a helpful note for the actor. I said, 'You can't play naïve, so forget about that', and her performance was much better. 'Naïve' is an adjective, not a verb, so you can't play it as an objective.

Mistake #2. Putting emotion before objective

On the stage there cannot be . . . action which is directed immediately at the arousing of a feeling for its own sake. To ignore this rule results only in the most disgusting artificiality. When you're choosing some bit of action, leave feeling and spiritual content alone.

An Actor Prepares, STANISLAVSKI

Stanislavski had this advice for stage actors almost one hundred years ago, and actors are still making the same mistakes today. Some actors cry and roll around on the floor, thinking that if they show a lot of emotion that will get them the role. The objective is not to show off your ability to express emotions or tears. If it's appropriate and the tears come, then good. Consider, however that sometimes in good storytelling, we don't need to see the character cry. If you're playing a character whose daughter has just died, you don't have to play sad. The audience knows you're sad. The audience probably just saw the scene before when she died. You need to play the character's needs. The sadness may drive the character's goal, but play the goal. When Anthony Hopkins played that wonderfully sad and repressed Mr. Stevens in *Remains of the Day*, he said, 'I just stood still. I didn't have to cry. I let the audience cry for me.'

There are exceptions to everything of course. When I worked with director Daniel Espinosa, he confessed to me that he just loves to see actors cry and motivated them to always go to the deepest place emotionally in every audition.

Things to remember from this chapter

- Make choices that answer the 'W'-questions.
- Relate your objectives to the author's intention.
- Devise at least two different choices for the role.
- When possible, make contrasting choices.
- Play objectives, not emotions or character.

4

Determine the stakes

Actors who get cast are actors who determine the stakes.

Determine the stakes

'What are the stakes?' Since teaching my classes in over twenty countries, I've come to realize that 'Raise the stakes' is an English phrase and sometimes is awkward to translate.

In French, it translates well, '*Quels sont les enjeux?*' In German, they would say, '*Was ist auf dem Spiel?*' (What are you playing for?) In one Turkish class I realized that it had been interpreted as 'What are the breaks?' (as in, when are we stopping to have coffee?). In Sarajevo, they thought I was speaking about sirloin.

Another way to ask the question is: What does the character have to lose? What risk is he/she taking? What does the character care about? The etymology of the phrase stems from poker. Stakes refers to the ante. What's in the pot? When you play your hand at cards, are you betting one dollar, seven dollars, or a million dollars? The more money in the pot, the more you sweat, and the higher the stakes.

Getting actors to think about stakes in a poker game is an apt metaphor because money is often at stake in a good screenplay. What else can be at stake? Love, honour, power or the highest stake of all: life verses death. The raised stake is the key ingredient missing in many of the auditions I see. Actors don't set their stakes high enough. They're betting only seven dollars when they should be betting a million.

Note the following sides we used to audition actors for one of the supporting roles in *Mission Impossible IV: Ghost Protocol*. A fake scene was written specifically for the audition since we never showed actors anything from the real script. So when actors asked, 'Tell me more about the character', I couldn't answer because I knew only as much as they knew from reading the scene. This is often the case with auditions on blockbuster films, but you know what? All the information you need is in the scene.

Strangely we didn't need to audition Tom Cruise, who in this scene is 'Brad' (Ethan Hunt). We were auditioning the role of 'Anton' (in the film, Leonid).

The following scene is similar to the one we used.

```
INT. SAFEHOUSE - NIGHT
            (Anton sits across from Brad. Long
                     beat.)


                      ANTON
        Will you beat my face in like your
        buddies?


                      BRAD
        Natalia Federof is six feet under,
        because of your little bank stunt.


                      ANTON
        I did nothing.


                      BRAD
        You'll never see the outside of a
        prison when we show the court these
        surveillance photos.

            (He shows photos to Anton. . .)


                      ANTON
        How can you prove? This man wears
        mask?
            (Brad then changes strategies and
            shows Anton a photo of his family.
            Anton's expression changes . . .)
```

> BRAD
> (pointing at Anton in the picture)
> This man isn't a bank robber or a
> murderer. Why'd you do it?
> > (Anton softens.)
>
> ANTON
> I am from a land where we fear
> police. Moscow Police, will flip
> everything against you.
>
> BRAD
> I'm not judging. You must have had a
> reason. We can help you if you
> talk . . .
>
> ANTON
> I get to US one month ago. My wife
> and daughter are supposed to follow
> when I get papers. But KGB watch my
> family so they can't leave. Getting
> them to the US is difficult task. Man
> offers to help me. Criminal man . . .
>
> BRAD
> Ivan Sidilski.
>
> ANTON
> Sidilski . . . He says he will kill
> my wife and daughter if I do not
> bring him ten thousand dollars more
> by Saturday . . .

So let's examine Leonid's (aka Anton's) stakes. It's all there, money (he robbed a bank and has to come up with ten thousand dollars), love (he loves his wife and daughter), and life (if he doesn't do as he's told, they'll kill his family).

In the film, the character played by Ivan Shvedov, never acted this scene specifically. This dialogue was never spoken, and Leonid was a mostly silent character, whose presence is pivotal to the plot. Yet in every scene, he had to play the high stakes even if silently. The Secret

Service comes to his home, and kidnaps his family before his eyes. He is blackmailed into going to Dubai to unlock the codes to the end-of-the-world device. Here the audience has to believe that Leonid is going to lose everything if he doesn't go. The life and death stakes of the scenes can guide the actor's choices in the audition. This is an audition in which you can 'go for the Oscar'. Life doesn't get too much worse than this character's. So make sure that you're betting a million.

Things to remember from this chapter

- Determine what game your character is playing; how much money is in the pot?

- Stakes can determine the intensity of the scene.

5

Tell the story

Actors who get cast are actors who tell the story.

For as many times as it is appropriate to take a risk and play high stakes, there are equally as many times when it's appropriate to simply tell the story. Sometimes the stakes are low and there is less money involved in the poker game. When the stakes are high, it's right to go for the Oscar. Other times, it is best to blend into the story and support someone else's high stakes. This is when storytelling comes in. The director wants you to tell his story, not pop out from it. David Mamet, in his book, *True and False*, defending the position of the writer, wants an 'uninflected performance' from the actor. In other words, he doesn't want the performer to mess up his text by acting too much. Trust that you are expressing enough, and that the chemistry of your persona, merging with the objective of the character, will tell the story. You don't have to do handstands for the role every time.

Remember that you are only telling one piece of the story. Film is ultimately a director's art, with him coordinating the elements – set, costume, sound, lighting design – and arranging them with an editor. These combined elements tell the story. Sergei Eisenstein was an early twentieth-century Russian director who originated the idea of a montage. He proved that the actor's performance by itself has no efficacy without the context of the film. He conducted an experiment in which he filmed an actor doing different reaction shots. First he instructed the actor to react is if he had just been brought a bowl of soup after not having eaten for a week. Then, in a separate scene, he directed him to react as a recently released prisoner, seeing birds in the sky for the first time in years. When the audience viewed the scenes, of course they couldn't tell what the actor was experiencing, proving that the acting alone cannot show thought – editing must. It's the scenes that are interspersed with the actor's reactions that tell the story. Let the text and your voice carry the scene. Keep it simple.

A friend of mine, a successful Broadway actor, got a small role in a film. When they were shooting his performance, the director said, 'Cut! You're just too interesting of an actor for this role.' In the end, he was cut out of the film, and another actor was hired. The director had found a polite way to tell him that he was making the stakes too high. This is also called over-acting. He was trying to make his character too important when the scene wasn't about him. He was used to playing the central character in theatre productions. In theatre too, however, there is a phrase called 'giving stage' (supporting another character) and 'taking stage' (playing your own high stakes). In film and TV this applies as well.

In TV series, for example, the guest characters often appear to support the lead stars. The director, not to mention the star (they are often producers) may prefer that the actor disappear into the story, giving a low stakes performance. So actors who take big risks and play too high a stake in the audition, may be perceived as a threat to the story.

On the ABC series, *Missing*, Ashley Judd's character is fighting for extremely high stakes – her son's life. He has gone missing while studying in Europe, and she suspects he was kidnapped due to her CIA past. When he doesn't call her back, she goes to her local police station in Maryland. We used the following scene to audition a day player, Detective Storch.

```
INT. POLICE STATION - DAY
Becca sits across from FRANK STORCH, a middle-
aged detective with a paunch and an ingrown
toenail that's killing him. Becca is focused,
but under that, frightened.

                    BECCA
        I've already alerted the American
        Embassy. I need you to file an official
```

report with both the Italian Police
and Interpol.

> DETECTIVE STORCH
> And say what exactly? You got a
> kid on his own in the most romantic
> city on Earth, and he hasn't called
> his mommy?

Becca scans his desk. Takes A PHOTO OF HIS
FAMILY and points to his LITTLE GIRL.

> BECCA
> What's her name?

> DETECTIVE STORCH
> Katie. Why?

> BECCA
> Katie hasn't called you in five days.
> She promised she would, and for a
> while she did. And then she just
> . . . stopped. She doesn't answer her
> phone. Or return your calls.

Storch looks at the photo, Katie's happy face.
Softens.

> DETECTIVE STORCH
> I'll file the reports.

> BECCA
> How long will that take?

> DETECTIVE STORCH
> On my end, right away. On theirs, who
> knows? It's Italy.

In this scene it's clear that Becca's stakes are much higher than Storch's. For him, it's just another day at the office. 'Throw it away', was my note to the auditioning actors. The producers, the director, Ashley Judd and everyone, including the audience, wants Detective Storch to disappear into the story. We don't want the scene to be about a man who is suffering from an ingrown toenail. It is obviously about Becca and her need to find her son. She uses her high *stakes* to manipulate him to see her side. In her journeys through Europe, she continues to play high stakes in search of her son, until the show is pulled from the air, but you get the point. Here the auditioning actor has to *give* stage rather than *take* it. This is what best serves the story.

So can we conclude that the day player, or supporting actor is always there to disappear and give stage to the star? No. There are short cameo roles when there is a lot at stake, and those can be the hardest roles to play. For example, in the feature film *Snowpiercer*, director Bong Joon-Ho forges his own distinctive style telling epic stories in which the star meets a series of important, often quirky, cameo characters who play high stakes parts in the hero's journey. For example, in *Host*, there are scenes in which the camera zooms in on the precise moment in which the monster is about to overtake a pedestrian. The actor must project extreme fear and terror in his eyes, the moment that comes right before death. The audience must believe that the actor believes he is about to die.

Actors are, above all, storytellers. When preparing for an audition on either stage or screen, make sure to ask:

- Where are we in the story?
- How can I as a performer best serve it?
- Who else is in the scene and am I giving stage or taking stage?

Things to remember from this chapter

- Remember that you are a storyteller.
- Trust that your uninflected performance, combined with objective and text will tell the story.
- Determine if you are giving stage or taking stage.
- Film is a director's medium. You don't have to tell the entire story yourself, just a small piece of it.

6

Act and react in the moment

Actors who are cast are actors who act and react in the moment.

Be flexible and open to spontaneity. Almost anything can happen at a casting. Don't be thrown by the unexpected. It may be that by the time you get there, the script has already changed and they've cut your role. It's also possible that you mistakenly got the wrong sides, or they realize you're better for another part so you get handed another set of sides. You need to be flexible and able to go with it. This is why it's important to exercise your cold reading skills.

This also means being open to a change in your interpretation. You might be playing a pyschotic lunatic, while the director sees the character as perfectly sane. It's great to make a bold choice, and directors respect that, even if it's the 'wrong' interpretation. You have to be prepared, however, to go in an entirely different direction, and actors bomb this all the time. An actor will do a nice performance initially, but then they cannot adapt to the director's ideas. Directors are on guard for actors who get stuck in preplanned line readings. They want the material to sound fresh and unrehearsed. Some actors over-prepare, carefully planning their intonation on each line, driving themselves into a fixed vocal pattern. Prepare enough to be stable, but not so much that you're inflexible. To plan your performance is to plan your death.

Sometimes the person who reads opposite of you at the casting is as inspiring as a piece of cardboard, reading each line with a dull monotonous voice. This could be intentional because they don't want to influence your performance. In these cases you have to work off of your own energy, or as Michael Caine says, 'If the other actor isn't giving you what you want, act as though they were.' Other times you get a reader who is giving you a performance on the other side because they want to elicit a certain response from you. If you've been rehearsing the scene in a particular way and then the person you are reading with suddenly shouts out one line unexpectedly, do not ignore it. React the way you think the character would react in this situation. As in theatre, audition performance should be a fluid, flowing, living entity. Part of what the director is testing is your ability to take directions. He might give you a crazy direction just to see if you'll go with it.

The director wants to know that you are listening to him. I once worked with a very good actor, who was close to getting the role of Ilsa on *Hellboy*. She thought it was her job to 'sell' the director her ideas for the role. The director, Guellermo Del Toro, had written the script and had a specific vision for how he wanted the role performed. Instead of listening to and incorporating his ideas, she clung to her own interpretation. She was not cast. A director wants an actor who listens. Once you're cast, over and over again, and become a star – then you'll get your chance to influence the script, but not in the audition. Come with your own ideas, but be willing to change them to adapt to the whims of the production.

Things to remember from this chapter

- Expect the unexpected.
- Stay flexible so you can change your interpretation.
- Listen and respond to the director.
- Don't expect inspiration from the reader.
- Respond to the reader if they are giving you a performance.

7

Play in the eyes

Actors who get cast are actors who play in the eyes.

> I have looked into your eyes with my eyes. I have put my heart near your heart.
>
> POPE JOHN XXIII

Film photographs thought. The thought is in the eyes. If there is one trick in film acting, it is to keep the acting in the eyes. When actors are mugging, or over-acting in the brow, one effective note is 'to channel the acting through the eyes, not in the face'. When you communicate with your eyes, think with your eyes, listen with your eyes, the camera will love you. Be like Medusa and kill with your eyes. The eye can become as large as eight feet wide on a big screen. When an actor concentrates on communicating with his eyes, the performance follows suit. Getting the brow unfurled is only a slight adjustment, and it's about awareness.

The LA theatre company, the Actors' Gang, followed by the now defunct New Crimes of Chicago, pioneered a very distinct Commedia Dell'Arte performance style in the 1980s, wherein the actor would face off directly with the audience, looking straight into an individual spectator's eyes. Their training sessions challenged actors to express strong levels of energy, directing emotions through the eyes and sending them to the audience. The New Crimes Commedia Dell'Arte was a highly physicalized form of theatre, accompanied by an insane, thumping rock and roll drumbeat. It seems unlikely that this style could be useful for film acting, which is grounded so fully in realism. Yet the founding members of the Actors' Gang and New Crimes, such as Tim Robbins, John Cusack and Jeremy Piven have gone on to have fantastically successful film acting careers. I believe that this was in part because they had so much practice with communicating with their eyes.

The form of theatre they practised they refer to as 'the style'. Original New Crimes member, Adele Robbins, says about her brother, 'Tim believes in the style and always returns to it. It informs everything.' I have adapted some of the training that I got from New Crimes members into exercises. Although I didn't know it while I was training, 'the style' offered some of the most helpful techniques that I've learned for film acting.

If acting in the eyes is something that doesn't come naturally to you, then join the club. Like anything in acting, it can be practised and improved. Learn to work with your eyes. Experiment in front of camera. Painters practise by drawing models in the studio, singers sing scales, dancers do pliés, yet there are people who think that without any training at all they can just get in front of camera and act. As the sculptor uses a chisel, so the actor has her eyes. They are your main tool. In an audition, be as generous as possible with your eyes, always turning them towards camera. Do not bury your eyes in the script, allowing us to see only your eyelids. Your eyelids are not interesting. Master cold reading techniques, that help you look up from the script. Doff the glasses, when possible. Wear contacts or do without whenever possible. As the Yiddish proverb goes, 'The eyes are the mirror of the soul.'

In his seminars to actors Michael Caine discusses the importance of the eyes in film acting; he suggests that actors get to know their leading eye. Everyone has one eye that is keener than the other. Learn which eye leads and cheat that eye towards the camera. For example, if it's your left eye, then focus to the right of camera.

About blinking

In a close-up, even a blink registers as a ten on the Richter scale. During my classes when we play back the scenes my actors often say, 'But I'm blinking too much.' Each actor is bothered by his own blinking on screen, even when the rest of the class doesn't notice. Michael Caine claims that he has trained himself not to blink during close-ups. But we all know that our eyes need moisture and that's why we blink, right?

I don't believe it is necessary for an actor to train himself not to blink. Editor Walter Murch has devoted considerable research to the blink. In his book *The Blink of an Eye*, he suggests that the blinking actor provides an opportunity for the editor to cut. He first noticed it when he was editing an early Coppola film, *The Conversation*. 'I kept finding that Gene Hackman would blink very close to the point where I had decided to cut.' So Murch then started to pay acute attention to when and why people blink. 'People will sometimes keep their eyes open for minutes at a time – at other times they will blink repeatedly – with many variations in between . . . Our rate of blinking is somehow geared more to our emotional state and to the nature and frequency of our thoughts.'

So sometimes when an actor thinks he blinks too much, he is picking up on his own discomfort with the role or performance. If you're focused on the role, the blinks will come at the right time and in the right abundance. Trust yourself and stay the course with making choices that help you to identify with the role.

Things to remember from this chapter

- Thought reads in the eyes.
- Keep the acting in the eyes and not in the forehead.
- Your eyes are your main tool, so learn to use them.

8

Possess an inner monologue

Actors who get cast are actors who possess an inner monologue.

When you foster an active and changing internal monologue, the eyes will be alive.

While 'less is more' is a good adage, doing 'less' can lead to the opposite extreme – dead face. Overacting is the camera's worst nightmare, but dead face is deadly. Dead face happens when an actor is not thinking in character, and the mind is not engaged – nice house but nobody's home. In other words, there is no inner monologue. Ironically this seems to happen most with stage actors who are afraid to overact, so instead they end up doing nothing.

Because many actors fear overacting, casting directors see a lot of safe and frankly dead auditions. Overacting is difficult to define but you know it when you see it. Film critics are too lazy to even type it, preferring to use the initials OTT (over the top). It does not necessarily mean doing 'too much' (whatever that is). If you consider some of the world's favourite actors, Robert de Niro and Jack Nicholson, for example, you will find that they do quite 'a lot'. Examine their performances. These successful actors manage to find stillness while their faces are alive with thought and intention.

Overacting is when an actor mugs (makes faces), and uses excessive gesture. It means that the actor is trying to 'show' the audience what a character is feeling. This performance is not grounded in truth and believability and this is poor acting in both film and theatre. The dreaded overacting can also happen when an actor pre-judges a character, or when they get themselves into a pattern of punctuating the lines, that become fake after a few reads. The antidote to both dead face and overacting is to develop and concentrate on the inner monologue of the character.

For a close-up, as the theory goes, all the actor has to do is think the inner monologue, and the viewer will know; the camera exposes all. Think the character's thought. In my classes, however, some actors have learned that thinking in character reveals nothing. Even though they insist that they've got an active inner monologue, when they watch the tape they see no light in their eyes, and no wheels turning in their head (which demonstrates the value of watching oneself on camera occasionally).

If your face is dead, then you've got to work harder to liven up your inner monologue. French film star Jeanne Moreau claims that, 'acting is not true to life, it is beyond', and that actors must 'not only listen but listen beyond'. On camera we don't have to speak louder than in life, but we may have to think louder. Here is an example from the script *Before Sunset,* written by Richard Linklater, Kim Krizan, Julie Delpy and Ethan Hawke.

```
8     EXT. GARDEN PATH STAIRWAY - AFTERNOON
They continue to walk/talk.


                    JESSE
          No, no, tell me the truth. Did we
          have problems that night?


                    CELINE
          I was kidding. We didn't even have
          sex anyway.


                    JESSE
          What? That's a joke, right?


                    CELINE
          No, we didn't. That was the whole
          thing.
```

                    JESSE
Of course we did.

                    CELINE
But we didn't. You didn't have a
condom and I never have sex without
one, especially if it was a one-night
thing. I'm extremely paranoid about
my health.

                    JESSE
I'm finding this very scary that you
don't remember what happened.

                    CELINE
You know what, I didn't write an
entire book, but I kept a journal and
I wrote the whole night in it. That's
what I meant by you idealizing the
night.

                    JESSE
                (a bit louder)
I even remember the brand of condom I
used.

                    CELINE
That's disgusting.

Walking by are an older couple with three kids.
They look back, a bit shocked.

                    JESSE
No, it isn't.

                    CELINE
All right, when I get home, I'll
check my journal from '94, but I know
I'm right.
                (a beat)

> Wait a minute. Was it in the cemetery?

> JESSE
> Noooo. We visited the cemetery during
> the day. It was in the park, very
> late at night.

> CELINE
> Wait a minute.

> JESSE
> Was it that forgettable? You don't
> remember, in the park?

> CELINE
> Wait a minute, I think you might be
> right.

> JESSE
> You're messing with me.

In this scene, Celine does more of the talking than Jesse, so it's acutely important for Jesse to keep his inner monologue going. If his inner monologue is 'I can't believe this. She doesn't remember having sex with me. I can't believe this. She doesn't remember having sex with me. I can't believe this. She doesn't remember having sex with me', then he's probably giving a pretty boring performance. Just as the choices on line readings are important, so are the choices on inner monologue and subtext, and the same rules apply. The camera loves contrast and change. The camera loves discovery. So the actor playing Jesse needs to spin an inner monologue that is not only active, but varied. Some of the different thoughts winding around in his head can be:

- I know we had sex and I'm undressing you with my eyes right now.

- Was I that awful in bed that you don't remember?

- Maybe we really didn't have sex and I just imagined it.

- You must be kidding!

Then finally –

– Thank God, she remembers!

If these types of varied thoughts are revolving, his performance will live and breathe.

If thinking in character isn't effective for you, then do whatever works. Dustin Hoffman says, 'The method is your method.' Billy Bob Thornton, while performing in *The Man Who Wasn't There*, spent a lot of time on screen without uttering a word. When asked what he was thinking about in his reaction shots, he glibly replied that he was thinking a lot about James Gandolfini's shoes. I'm also reminded of Wim Wenders' film *Wings of Desire*, in which angels overhear the inner thoughts of humankind. While trailing actor Peter Falk on a film set in Berlin, they picked up on him thinking, 'I wonder what I'll have for dinner. Maybe some spaghetti with marinara sauce.' Nobody really cares what your process is. Your method, whether it is thinking the character's thoughts, or thinking about lunch is what works for you. A solid bet is to activate the face and the eyes with a charged and changing inner monologue. Dead face is deadly.

Things to remember from this chapter

- Possess an inner monologue.

- An inner monologue is the antidote to both dead face and overacting.

- The camera loves contrast and discovery.

- Do whatever works for you to create an active and alive performance in which the wheels in your head are turning.

9

Commit to the scene

Actors who get cast are actors who commit to the scene, not the lines in the scene.

- What happens in the scene?
- What does the character want?

It is more important to nail *what happens* in the scene, than to perform a perfectly memorized line reading. I have seen actors who become so obsessed with flawlessly reciting the lines that they miss the point of the scene. It is not interesting to watch an actor without a script in his hand struggle to recall lines. Remember that the audition is not a memory test. The more familiar you are with the text, the easier it will be to act, but keeping the script in hand is accepted in the USA and the UK. We all know how easily the lines flow when you're rehearsing it in your bedroom, but somehow they all fall out of your head when you're at the audition. Holding the sides is a kind of security blanket and it reminds us that this is not a finished performance, it's a work in progress.

If you get a word wrong, don't point out your mistake. Mistakes can result in fresh discovery. Too many times, I have seen actors want to stop the scene and repeat it merely because they flubbed a line. You need to behave at the casting the way you behave on set. Cover and continue. It took the crew hours to set up the shot, so you don't make them stop the reel for a line error. The editor can cut around it. Part of what we're testing in the audition is your ability to concentrate and get through the scene. Therefore, stay in the scene, even if your pants are on fire, until you hear 'cut!'.

We are not just interested in you saying the lines perfectly. We're interested in what you bring to the role. We want to see your interpretation, your energy, your choices, your dynamic. Don't worry about pronunciation. When we were casting *Dune*, actors had to stumble over words like 'Ibn Qirtaiba' and 'Ikhut-Eigh' – language specific to Frank Herbert's sci-fi world. At the auditions, it was a source of stress for actors, but we didn't care about it. We knew that they would pick it up on set where we had a dialogue coach. If you go up on a few lines, you will be forgiven if you are playing the character's actions and objectives. Pull us into the story, and it might not even matter what words are coming from your mouth.

In a comedy, 'committing to the scene' means telling the jokes properly. In this case, if you don't get the wording right on a punch line, the joke doesn't work. In a comedic scene, your job is to figure out the jokes and tell them. A carefully planned joke doesn't work with lots of 'ums' and 'ers'. It needs to be told concisely. Sometimes the writer is at the casting. So if Peter Morgan is in the room, get it right. You want to do the script as much justice as you can. The audition is generally not the time to intentionally change the text.

Things to remember from this chapter

- Memorize the lines if you wish, but more importantly memorize what is important in the scene.

- Casters are more interested in what you bring to the role than your perfect recitation of the lines.

- Keep the scene going even if you do fluff a line.

10

Stake a claim on the role, take a risk

Actors who get cast stake a claim and take a risk.

Actors who come in and own the part are the people we have confidence in. They're the ones we're happy to present to a director, because they'll make us look good.

JANET HIRSHENSON, casting director,
from her book *A Star is Found*

This is your time. Remember you are entitled to be at that audition. You were invited, and you deserve to be there. Take your time, own the space, and stake a claim to the role. The actors who are humble and enter with the attitude of 'You, oh great director, have granted me this favour of your time, so I, little actor, will hurry', are not the ones who get the job. Directors feel comfortable with self-possessed actors, who are confident in their abilities. Ask questions if you have any, and take a beat before you start the scene to focus yourself. Treat casting directors and directors as collaborators and peers.

Staking a claim means being physically and psychically prepared. Do what you need to do beforehand to warm up. No one will warm you up at the audition. I'm shocked when I see an actor reading a newspaper in reception before performing an unprepared audition.

Sometimes actors want to walk in the door already in character. This is one approach but you have to be flexible because some casting directors like to chat first. If this is your case, inform the receptionist that you're ready to go right into it so that he can 'announce' you that way. Most casting directors will respect this approach.

The actor who gets cast is the actor who commands the room, and boldly squares off with the material. When actor, Petr Vanek, read for the role of Felipe, the bellboy in *Last Holiday*, he had a scene in which Georgia (Queen Latifah's character) asks him, 'Did I over-tip you?' The scripted reply is 'Yes.' Instead he replied 'No'(with a sneaky sparkle in his eye, like he didn't want to return the super-big tip) and director Wayne Wang gave a hearty laugh. Petr was commanding the scene and the attention of everyone in the room. He wasn't in fact playing the lines, he made another choice – but he made it work with the scene. No one cared that he read the wrong line because he owned the scene, and was claiming the role. He got it.

Producer Frank Marshall discusses this concept in an interview about *The Sixth Sense*. For the character of the disturbed boy's mother, director M. Night Shyamalan wanted an actor with an authentic Philadelphian accent, but he ended up casting an Australian. 'There's a moment when an actor comes in they claim the role', said Marshall. 'And Toni Collette did that . . . she just got it. She knocked us out.'

Come into the audition as if to rehearse; you already have the role. That's what the movie stars do. At a rehearsal, you can take risks and play with the material.

> You're only as good as the chance that you take.
>
> AL PACINO

There are far too many actors who play it safe. Don't be afraid to take the scene somewhere. Remember that we're seeing hundreds of auditions. There will be many actors who can technically act the scene. But what do they bring to it? A good place to take risks is in the places where the scene changes. Dare to hit the transitions. Most scenes have a turning point, a place where the scene hinges or the dynamic changes. The scene needs to go from A to Z, not A to B. The camera loves contrast, and change.

I went to see Mozart's Opera, *The Marriage of Figaro*. The singer who sang the famous 'Aprite un po' aria performed this biting number about the treachery of women with the passion of a plumber fixing a drain. I thought to myself, 'He's singing it perfectly but why do I want to fall asleep?' He had a lovely, trained operatic voice, and he hit every note with a measured expertise. But there was no love in it. There is something thrilling about an artist, an actor, a singer, an athlete who dares to walk out on the tightrope without a net. Dare to climb, to jump and to soar.

Things to remember from this chapter

- Claim the role.
- Warm yourself up before you step through the door.
- Play the scene like you've already got the role and you're at the first rehearsal.
- Take a risk; too many actors play it safe.
- The camera loves discovery and change.

11

Listen

Actors who get cast are actors who listen.

No man ever listened himself out of a job.

CALVIN COOLIDGE

You can talk your way into a corner, but you can't ever listen too much. There are two types of listening that must take place. The first is for the *actor* to listen and respond to the director's notes. The second is that the *character* must listen and react in the moment to the actor who is reading the other part. He is your opponent in a tennis game and if you don't listen you won't know where the ball is.

One unfortunate but common mistake is speaking the lines very animatedly but listening like a zombie, simply waiting for the other actor to finish his line, or even worse anticipating what the other will say. The camera is unforgiving of this error. If you haven't had much time with the text, the temptation is to read the other character's lines instead of listening to them. Keep your finger on the text and listen to the reader, then find your line again. It's OK if there is a slight delay. Actors who don't listen are often text obsessed, so afraid of dropping a line that they just stare at the script. It's more important to listen and react to the other character than it is to get the line exactly correct. (Please see my exercises in Part Six.)

The next time you watch a film, observe how many times the camera is on the actor who is listening. It's there a lot. Director and teacher Patrick Tucker in *Secrets of Screen Acting* notes that 'The viewer does not want to know how the [speaking] person feels about something she has just said, they want to know what the other person feels about it; this is the unknown in the scene.' Listening is interesting. Listening also entails reacting, internally if there are no lines, and externally if there is a line. You may be forming your answer in your head half-way into the other actor's speech. Listen with your eyes. Listening and reacting in character is at the heart of effective screen acting.

In the CBS TV film, *Hitler: The Rise of Evil*, we cast the late Patricia Netzer as Sophie Gerlich almost entirely based on her listening skills. Patricia prepared a self-taped scene and sent it to us. What sold the producer most was the part of her audition in which she simply put the camera on herself, and listened, silently reacting to a conversation between her husband and Hitler. The director knew that he would always have a place to put the camera, with this actor on set. If you are a good listener, you will get more screen time. In the words of the Greek philosopher Plutarch, 'Know how to listen, and you will profit even from those who talk badly.'

Things to remember from this chapter

- Listen to the director's notes.

- Listen to the other character in the scene.

- The camera loves a good listener.

- Your reaction to the other actor is as important as your line delivery.

12

Make your own work

Actors who get cast are actors who make their own work.

An actor comes home to find his wife bruised and badly beaten. He huddles down to his crying spouse and desperately demands, 'Who did this to you? I'll kill him.'

'It was . . .' she weakly tries to answer.

'Was it the mail man?' he interrupts, 'I always thought he was suspicious.'

'No, no . . .' she stammers, trying to find the words.

'Was it the gardener? That swine!'

'No, no . . . It was your agent.'

'My agent stopped by?' he asks hopefully.

Don't be an actor who sits and waits by the phone for your agent to call. This is a miserable way to live. If the phone isn't ringing, staring at it won't help. Actors need to be proactive. One of my teachers used to say, 'It's a poor dog who can't wag his own tail.' There are so many ways to get out there and wag your own tail, especially in the age of the viral video.

Once an actor complained to me that he wasn't succeeding because casting directors ignored him. He said 'The casting directors have control over my career and whether I make it or not.' This is absolutely not true. Take the power back. You are the only one who is in charge of whether you succeed or not.

This is the most valuable advice that I teach my actors at the Prague Film School. Make your own work. If no one is casting you, if there is no one making a film or play with a role that is right for you, then make one for yourself. Write a play about you, directed by you, produced by you, with you in mind. Create the perfect role for yourself. If you don't like to write, then find material. There are plenty of good plays out there. When you are doing theatre, 'push yourself and work with good people', advises casting director Meg Liberman. You will learn from your co-stars. Not only are you attracting possible agents and casters, you are also honing your skills and getting better with each performance.

If your city doesn't host a fringe festival, then start one. Fringe festivals are full of that sizzling energy created by hundreds of talented actors who are frothing at the mouth to work. These actors are seizing the moment, practising their craft. As nineteenth-century playwright, Friedrich Schiller said, '. . . he who has lived the best of his own age will live for many ages to come.' It is these performances that will burn themselves into the minds of viewers, not just the big blockbuster films. Stars who got their start at the Edinburgh Fringe Festival, for example, include Jude Law, Gerard Butler, Hugh Grant, Ricky Gervais and Rachel Weisz. There was a time when these actors weren't famous and were noticed for the first time, but they didn't do it by sitting at home.

Stephen Berkoff confesses that he composed his now famous adaptation of Franz Kafka's story *Metamorphosis* when he was out of work and sick of waiting for the phone to ring. *Metamorphosis* was nothing more than a talent vehicle for Berkoff – playing a cockroach of all things. Now Berkoff can languidly wait by the phone. This time, in addition to getting acting offers, he's waiting for his agent to call and report on the royalties he earns when the play continues to be produced as a star vehicle for other actors, like Mikhail Baryshnikov. If you create a good role, other actors will want to play it too.

If your phone isn't ringing with film offers, then take the reins into your own hands, and make a film yourself. 'But wait a minute,' you're thinking, 'don't I need millions of dollars to make a film?' The answer is no. All you need is a camera (a simple digital video camera will do), a computer with an editing program, and a lot of ideas, energy and enthusiasm. Choose something that matters to you and find your voice to express it through film.

There are independent film festivals bursting out of every city. If no one accepts your film, then you can pop it on YouTube. There are online film festivals and even smart phone film festivals. The Internet bars no one from promoting their work. Unknown actors are able to attract agents, and auditions for top-scale roles when they produce good online work.

The film *Good Will Hunting* launched the careers of Matt Damon and Ben Affleck, and it was written by – guess who? Matt Damon and Ben Affleck. Some of the world's best drama has come from actors who were writing material for themselves to perform. The great bard himself, Willy Shakespeare, was an actor.

Vin Diesel didn't know that he was on a straight course to action hero superstardom when he made his own film, *Multi-Facial* in 1994. The film, about multiculturalism and identity, was close to his heart. He made the film because he had a passion to express himself. That $3,000 film was accepted for the acclaimed Cannes Film Festival in 1995, eventually catching the attention of Steven Spielberg, who offered him a role in *Saving Private Ryan*. Other actors who started by writing their own material include Owen Wilson, Ben Stiller, Steve Martin, Tina Fey and Emma Thompson.

If you feel like producing or writing isn't your bag, then team up with someone else. When you're doing a play or a web series, you've got a product that you can invite casting directors and agents to see. Collect reviews from your play and you've got material to send out and post on your website. If it's a short film, you can send the whole film, or edited scenes of your best work can go on a show reel and website.

TV is another area that actors are breaking into on their own. The Internet allows actors to create their own channels and networks. Lena Denham pioneered her way into TV by first creating, producing and directing the film *Little Furniture* (starring herself). This was a small ($65,000) family-made film, in which she, her sister and her mother all played themselves. *Little Furniture* attracted Judd Apatow who then helped her develop it into the multi-award winning HBO TV series *Girls*, in which she plays the self-obsessed Hannah Horvath.

Other actors have pushed themselves ahead by generating their own web series and YouTube videos that go viral. Olga Sergeevna

Karavaeva is an actor who grew up in Russia, and trained as a circus performer. When she moved to Los Angeles, she started innovating YouTube videos, under the name of Olga Kay, that boosted her career when they went viral. She now makes a living by hosting several different channels. It should be noted that she makes a living playing herself mostly, so this may not be every actor's goal.

Brandon Hardesty came to public attention when he created videos based on mainstream films in which he played (parodied) all the different characters. These hilarious YouTube clips attracted the attention of talk show host Jimmy Fallon, who featured him in one of his shows. Even better, producer Edwin Marshal cast him directly in a film called *Bart Got a Room*, and he also landed a Beverly Hills manager and agent. Lisa Donovan is another brilliant producer/actor who promotes her own work under the name LisaNova. Her amusing impressions led her to a contract with MadTV and now she works regularly.

Even if a self-generated web series doesn't bring you big fame, it can at least qualify you for SAG (Screen Actors Guild) eligibility. Lack of union membership bars actors from auditioning for many projects. Because the Alliance of Motion Picture and Television Producers now recognize the legitimacy of new media, non-union actors can now shortcut to SAG eligibility via their work on web series. This has resulted in SAG providing provisions for non-union talent to join the union through independent new-media projects.[1] The trick is to produce a series, featuring yourself with other union members. Web series are a way to pad your resumé as well.

Not every actor will end up being an Internet star, but you can still use YouTube and vlogging to promote yourself and develop a following. I encourage my students at the Prague Film School to keep vlogs and create web series that feature them as main characters. Vlogging can be part of your actor website. Instead of blogging (writing what's happening in your career), why not vlog it? Then potential casters can see how you are on screen, and get a sense of what types of roles you might play.

Many actors who bounced sky-high from the success of viral videos are comedians. Everyone loves to laugh and the short YouTube

---

[1] SAG rules regularly change, so double check current rules.

format lends itself well to jokes. Not all actors are funny, but there are other types of videos that you can create. Storytelling is a wonderful form. The Moth is a grassroots storytelling organization that capitalizes on the raw power of the individual standing on stage and telling a personal story. It attracts viewers like a moth to a flame (hence the name). Themoth.org is the website that broadcasts audio podcasts of these stories. Actors can showcase their storytelling skills by participating in a city near them. I would love to see more actors using the storytelling format to promote their careers.

It's important to know that casting directors are indeed seeking and finding fresh talent from internet video clips. This works both ways, however. A bad video (either viral or not) can really hurt you. There is one rather well-known actor who started creating and posting his own off-beat, alternative videos that don't appeal to all tastes. I know that this put some producers off when I suggested him for a role. Exercise caution and do your best to manage and control your own content.

> ### Ideas for vlogging (video blogging) and self-generated videos
>
> - Web series starring yourself as the main character.
> - Storytelling videos (see themoth.org).
> - Helpful advice for other actors in your community, such as acting tips, books you've read, videos you've seen.
> - News and information on your actor website about projects you're working on.

Things to remember from this chapter

- Learn to create work for yourself.
- Don't sit by the phone, giving all the power to casting directors.
- Create a film, play, or web series starring you.

- Create a YouTube or Vimeo Channel featuring your work.
- Vlog regularly on your website.

'You are your business. You have to do everything you can to support your business. Your agent can't teach you the juggling skills, riding or singing or whatever. They can get you through the door and can say "I've got an actor who can play the oboe", but they can't play it for you, so you have to do everything to make you, your business, as wide-ranging as possible. And I would also say if you're not working, please don't sit around being out of work. Go spend time with children or do something else so that when you come to a meeting, you're not so nervous and thinking, "God, I haven't worked in six months", and you can say "I took six months off because I wanted to help handicapped children", and suddenly you become very interesting.'

The late EMMA STYLE, casting director, UK

PART TWO

Actor marketing in the Internet age

13

Archetype as branding

When I trained at the National Theatre Institute, I performed a monologue for casting directors who visited the school. I chose Phoebe's speech when she's rejected by Ganymede (Rosalind disguised as a man) in *As You Like It* because I thought it was funny. ('Think not I love him though I ask for him.') The casting director looked at me and said, 'But you're Rosalind, not Phoebe.' She was right – I didn't get it. I couldn't play the dumb, comic country girl. I had to play the sophisticated city slicker. In *Little Miss Sunshine* Olive Hoover wanted so much to be a beauty queen, but she couldn't see that she wasn't like the pornographically pretty girls around her at the competition. There was no doubt, however, that she was the most extraordinary girl there. Know your archetype.

Actors want to play all roles, and perhaps they can at some point in their careers. If you want to be employable, however, remember that casting directors, producers and writers think in terms of characters and types. In psychology and mythology it's called archetype. In marketing it's called branding. The more competitive the market, the more an actor has to brand himself, to make himself special and unique in his 'product niche'.

While, on the one hand, I would say that some of the most brilliant casting choices have deliberately gone against type, there is nothing wrong with typecasting. Remember the second part of the word 'typecast' is 'cast'. Actors often resist the idea of 'types' because it reminds them of stereotypes, which indicate a derogatory over-simplification of character. Archetypes, however, have existed in show business for centuries, starting with the masked Greek dramas, to Commedia del'Arte to Shakespeare to the sitcoms of today.

An archetype refers to the original model of a person, or in the words of psychologist Karl Jung, a 'symbolic figure' or a 'collective representation' of a person, drawn from 'the universal symbolism' that we share. Audiences connect with archetypes.

Vin Diesel, who is racially and ethnically nebulous, made a film about his frustration with typecasting. He produced, directed and acted in *Multi-Facial* early in his career, or rather before he *had* a career. It was about an actor who continually fell between the cracks at auditions for Italian-Americans, Hispanics, or African Americans. He never got the job. In the process, Diesel branded himself, created his own character and type, which ironically has made him famous. The lesson is to know thyself and what you can play well. If no one is casting you, cast yourself and show us how to cast you. Once you start getting work, you can branch out, and develop work in other archetypes.

Here are examples of archetypes from films we know:

Epic archetypes

The Innocent – Dorothy in *The Wizard of Oz*
Orphan – Oliver Twist
Warrior – Superman, James Bond, Bourne
Caregiver – Hanna the Nurse in *The English Patient*
Creator – Aslan in *Narnia*
Seeker – Harry Potter, Luke Skywalker
Lover – Will Turner in *Pirates of the Caribbean*
Destroyer – The Wicked Witch in *The Wizard of Oz*
Ruler – Queen Elizabeth I in *Elizabeth*, Henry in *Henry V*
Magician – Gandalf in *Lord of the Rings*
Sage – Ben Obi Wan Kenobi in *Star Wars*
The Child Man – Peter Pan
Fool – David Brent (Ricky Gervais) in *The Office* (British) or Michael
    Scott (Steve Carrell) in *The Office* (US)
The Fanciful Aunt – Mary Poppins and Aunti Mame

Here are more general archetypes listed with famous actors who play them.

Family archetypes

The father – Liam Neeson
The mother – Brenda Blethyn

Story archetypes

The hero – Will Smith
The maiden – Kristin Stewart
The wise old man – Morgan Freeman
The witch or sorceress – Tilda Swinton
The trickster – Steve Buscemi
The child man – Zach Galifianakis
The wimp – Woody Allen, Jesse Eisenberg, Michael Cera
The rake – Any James Bond actor, Jon Hamm in *Mad Men*, Warren Beatty

Archetypes have morphed to include these more specific types that appear in today's film, TV and commercial projects:

MALE	FEMALE
Computer Geek	Bimbo
Footballer	Football Wife
Bouncer	Cheerleader
Rapper	Feminist
Hustler	Bag Lady
Mob Boss	Mafia Wife
The Stag Night Bloke	The Trafficked Sex Worker
Metro Sexual	The Butch Female
The Drag Queen	The Dumb Blond

MALE OR FEMALE	CHILDREN
Doctor	Precocious Child
Lawyer	Abused Child
CEO	Skateboarder
Night Clubber	Nerd
Junkie	Fat Kid
Couch Potato	Popular Kid

It's useful for actors to identify their archetypes, also called primary types, casting brackets or niches. When you put your product on the marketplace, customers want to know what they're buying. You'll use your archetypes as part of your branding process. Knowing your archetypes helps you select an image for a headshot. Choosing a primary archetype doesn't mean that you have to stick with this one type only. Look at Tilda Swinton. I have listed her as the witch archetype because of her role in *Narnia*, but she just as deftly played the delicate, vulnerable mother in *I Am Love*. Archetypes will morph and change during an actor's lifetime. Archetypes also change over time. Kristin Scott Thomas made the jump from young lover (early in her career) to wise mother. Judy Dench once played the fragile, virginal Juliet and now she plays the Queen Warrior. You can shoot a variety of headshots that are within your range and present specific ones when you audition for different roles.

Bonnie Gillespie, author of *Self-Management for Actors*, suggests watching 'TV, commercials, films and plays with a notepad . . . to see what types are out there to be able to determine what primary type you are.' Look at your CV and see if there is a trend. Are you playing mostly the naughty girl, the prostitute, or the mother, or nurse? Think about working actors who are playing the roles that you would play, and investigate how these actors present themselves. If you struggle to fit in, then follow in the footsteps of performers like Vin Diesel who created his own archetype.

Knowing your archetypes is part of knowing yourself, as a person and as an artist. I once taught a very competent American actor who had a lovely warm quality, and easily fit in the range of lover, father, teacher, businessman, etc. When I was casting a Russian mafia hit man role, he wrote and asked if he could audition for it (what, huh?!) I was fairly shocked that he didn't know himself well enough to know that role was well out of his range. Conversely, don't limit yourself too much, by not trying at some point to face the challenge and push past the archetypes within your comfort zones. I once assigned an actor an aristocratic character and he said, 'I only play lower-class roles.' He gave up a great chance to stretch himself. In Part One, I discuss examples of actors who come to an audition believing they can't play a role, even when the casting director has invited them. Challenge yourself to grow, and allow your archetypes to shift, as you advance through your career.

Things to remember from this chapter

- An archetype refers to the original model of a person.
- Identify the archetypes that you are likely to play to help guide your marketing choices.

14

Winning headshots

All photos are accurate. None of them is the truth.
RICHARD AVEDON, photographer

A headshot is a neutral photo of the actor's face, and it's important because it is often the first thing a casting director sees. A good headshot is an accurate photo, spun to get you the most work possible. That does not mean spinning the photo so that you look a thousand times better than in real life. The biggest mistake that actors make is presenting themselves inaccurately, namely, their headshots don't look like them. Casting directors want the person who walks into the room to look exactly like their headshot. That means a current shot, with your hair, eyebrows, beard, teeth, reasonably the same as it will be on the day of the audition.

Guidelines for headshots

A headshot isn't a photo. It's a marketing tool. Use it to 'show us how to cast you'.
BONNIE GILLESPIE, *Self-Management for Actors*

A successful headshot will:

1   *Look exactly like you.* This can't be emphasized enough. CSA
Casting Directors agree that the most important aspect of the
headshot is that it looks like the actor. Everyone wants to look
like their best self, so you're not going to portray yourself as
you would be getting out of bed on New Year's morning.
Headshot photographer Natasha Merchant says, 'a good
headshot captures the person looking exactly as they would
if you caught them walking down the street on a very
good day'.

> When I want to photograph someone, what it really means is that
> I'd like to know them. Anyone I know, I photograph.
>
> ANNIE LEIBOVITZ

2   *Reveal the actor's personality.* We should *know* you in your
photo. I've emphasized that the actor's unique style,
presence, personality, chemistry is what interests casting
directors the most. One recalls the scene in *Zoolander*, in
which Ben Stiller, playing a model, demonstrates his silly
poses, like 'blue steel', for photo shoots. This is a great
example of what *not* to do for a headshot session. You want
to look as natural, and relaxed as possible so that inimitable
thing that makes you *you* is revealed. The idea that certain
aboriginal people won't allow their photo to be taken for fear
of losing their soul, may have some relevance in as much
as a good picture will capture the essence and humanity
of that person.

3   *Feature active, thinking eyes.* While I advise *against* looking
into camera at an audition, shooting a headshot is the
opposite story. The eyes should look directly into the lens.
Just as film acting is based on expressing and communicating
through the eyes, a headshot should reflect a thought
process. The eyes should express intention without pulling a
face. Many headshot photographers use the focus technique
of honing in sharply on the eyes, while subtly softening out

towards the edges of the face so that the eyes draw in the viewer. During your photo session think about what you want to communicate to the viewer. Tell the camera you love it with your eyes. Tell the camera you want to kill it. Think of a line that a character who you want to play would say and say that to the camera.

4   *Suggest an archetype.* The best headshots are neutral, but will suggest an archetype that will help casters understand how to cast you. I do an exercise in my marketing seminars in which actors post their headshot and the class suggests what archetypes best suit them. One actor got suggestions like 'mob boss', 'criminal', and 'CIA spy'. Yet he had a warm, friendly personality, often playing the father or best friend. Since he never played these hard man types, the headshot was causing him to get called in for the wrong roles. He learned that his shot was not accurately representing his range of archetypes, and so he hired another photographer and re-shot.

5   *Archetype headshots.* Can you have more than one headshot? Yes, you can include many headshots in your gallery and keep special ones for special roles. Some actors keep separate 'commercial' photos for commercial work (see the examples from Cengis and Vanessa).

Sample headshots

James Babson (and his photographer, Lesley Bohm), share some examples of headshots. Because I know James, I know that all of these photos represent him accurately. Simply put, each photo looks like him and when he walks into the audition, no caster will be surprised or teed off. Each shot spins him slightly differently. If there is a specific role that James is going up for, either he or his agent can choose the appropriate shot to present.

Headshot #1 is James' 'key' photo (see photo 1). It's the one he posts on IMDb and his website, etc. It's a good neutral shot that allows a casting director to imagine him in a lot of different roles.

PHOTO 1
Photographer: Lesley Bohm

Headshot #2 is also a good shot but it takes the caster in a more specific direction (see photo 2). From this photo, I would cast him as the bad guy, the slightly edgy cop, the mafia henchman, the snarky advertising executive or that rascal of a boyfriend who just might cheat on you. It's still neutral but slightly meaner. The photographer has also chosen to display this one in landscape style rather than portrait. This is a trend now in North America, to tip the photo on its side. Landscape is considered acceptable. Just as a personal aside, however, I prefer portrait dimension. When we are casting we use 'casting boards', in which we post printed photos under each character's name. If some are in portrait and some are in landscape, the photos are just a bit harder to fit.

PHOTO 2
Photographer: Lesley Bohm

Headshot #3 (see photo 3) is the photo that James uses for commercial jobs. While it doesn't fit into the classic 'toothy smile' commercial headshot, it is a bit lighter, more open, more welcoming. Here we can see him as the guy next door, a suburban dad, our friendly doctor. We can imagine him selling lawn mowers.

PHOTO 3
Photographer: Lesley Bohm

Headshot no-nos

While I maintain that there is an exception to every rule, I would advise against the following:

1   *Heavily airbrushed photos.* Show us what you really look like, warts and all. We might want the warts. (A cold sore that isn't normally part of your facial landscape warrants a slight airbrush.)

2   *Lots of tooth.* While you do want to show some teeth for commercial shots, full on toothy smiles are a general no-no for a key neutral headshot. You may have a separate one for commercials (see Larissa Vereza's example, photo 4).

Selling to your market

Brazilian actor Larissa Vereza had to change her headshot when she changed markets. The first shot was an ideal marketing tool for her in Brazil (see photo 4). When I visited actors in Rio de Janeiro and São Paulo, I noticed this rightaway about their headshots; everyone was smiling! In fact, everyone in Brazil was smiling a lot. They're happy people down there in that tropical paradise.

PHOTO 4
Photographer: Lucio Luna

Normally I recommend that actors avoid showing a toothy smile in a headshot if they are marketing themselves for serious work in the US. The Brazilian shot is more a commercial shot. It sells the toothpaste. So she could still use it in the US if she is specifically up for a commercial.

The new photo that she had done in the US is more neutral and appropriate for the American market (see photo 5). There is an openness and vulnerability in the eyes. We could cast her as a romantic lead or an action hero.

PHOTO 5
Photographer: Matt Stasi

Rules for headshots

1   *Hands*. Keep hands out of the shots. (I don't ever want to see a picture of a girl with her finger in her mouth again. Save it for *Penthouse*.)

2   *Props*. Keep the shot simple. Use of too many props or gimmicks clutters the image. (Trust that we'll understand that you can play an academic without holding a stack of books, for example.)

3   *Specific backgrounds*. Keep the background as neutral and non-specific as possible. Let the viewer imagine you in different locations.

4   *Overly stylized photos*. Make sure that the photographer's style doesn't overpower the image. Remember that the headshot is a marketing tool for *you*, not the photographer.

5   *Headshots without name or contact information*. I know this sounds obvious, but I have too many unknown headshots floating around in my file. If you don't staple your CV to the back of your photo, at least stamp on your website, or agency contact info. If you are sending your photo as an attachment, please label it properly (i.e. with your name, not a number) so I can find it on my computer once I download it.

Styles of headshots

When selecting your headshot, consider to what market you are presenting. There are different trends in the US and the UK, but the industry standards in each country are becoming more similar. Only a few years ago, you saw only black and white used in London. Colour photographs are now widely used in the UK as well, especially since so many London actors are working 'across the pond'. In Europe, it's less standardized and I've seen a diversity of choices. Often an agency will make their own rules and standardize the presentation of their talent pool. The most important thing is not to worry too much about following rules, but rather presenting yourself professionally and accurately.

Headshot #6 (see photo 6) is the neutral key shot that Cengiz Dervis can use to market himself for a variety of roles. From this picture, I could cast him as a soldier, a lover, the guy next door or the baddie. Cengiz is half-Irish and half-Turkish Cypriot. In this photo, he's bringing forward his Irish side.

PHOTO 6
Photographer: David at People Portraits

In the second photo (see photo 7), Cengiz is obviously presenting a very specific archetype. This is definitely not a photo that an actor should use as his key photo. It's too limiting and he is not looking directly at camera. In fact, it could even be a production still. It's an ideal shot to put in his actor's gallery on his website. Cengis is an actor with stunt training so it suggests him for the action parts. While it's not the only role he wants to play, there are many roles written for Middle Eastern actors of this terrorist archetype. So it's a smart move on his part if he wants to work. A working actor is a happy actor.

PHOTO 7
Photographer: Graham Cantwell

The UK market

In the last release of my book, I was bemoaning the fact that British talent almost invariably displayed themselves in black and white. I'm delighted to see that British actors and agents have now discovered colour photography and are starting to join the rest of the world. London actor Lara Rossi had her headshots done in both colour and in black and white (see photos 8 and 9).

They are both excellent shots that look like her (with her hair

PHOTO 8
Photographer: Wolf Marloh, Camera Press London

PHOTO 9
Photographer: Wolf Marloh, Camera Press London

exactly as it was when this book went to press) and her soulful brown eyes pierce the lens of the camera. I met Lara while working on the *Crossing Lines* TV series, in which she played a tough, undercover cop. We often find her aiming a pistol. This first photo (photo 8) would get her more of those jobs. When she was trying to decide which shot to use, she considered what roles she was getting – the strong woman, the cop. I asked her what archetype she wanted to play, and she felt ready for a change (photo 9).

So Lara decided to use this second photo as her key headshot instead of the first. The second picture is similar but slightly more vulnerable. While normally I might advise actors not to display photos with the mouth open, this one works for Lara in this instance when she's spinning her archetype a bit differently. We can definitely imagine her playing the romantic lead from this softer, second photo.

CSA members prefer colour photos. A colour photo provides more information. In casting it's important to know if someone has red hair, or blue eyes. I dislike the strange stylized cropping techniques that US photographers are using now, where the actor isn't centred, or fully displayed. It's common sense to keep the actor in full view, rather than presenting them creatively. Use your own judgement, and keep in mind that there are no absolute rights and wrongs.

Sending your headshot

Professional presentation means sending one primary image to a casting director when auditioning for a specific role. It is fine to keep a few different headshots, earmarking specific looks for different jobs. Actors may shoot separate headshots for commercials, straight drama and musical theatre. Choose the image that fits the role. Don't confuse us with too many different looks. For example, do not even *think* of sending a composite with 15 different shots – in a nurse's outfit, with your dog, wearing glasses, making a funny face, with your hair blowing in a wind machine, etc. If you're responding to a general call where the role is unspecified or if you're applying to an agency, then you may send more than one photo. When sending two photos, I want the second photo to provide more or different information and a full body shot will do that. I urge actors to include photos that show their full form, or at least from the waist up.

Choosing and working with your photographer

I hope it goes without saying that you should hire a professional. Yes, your Uncle Jeffrey may take great photos and offer to do it for free, but the art of shooting a professionally accepted headshot is a very specific skill. Show us that you are serious about your career by making the investment. When choosing your photographer, it's not enough to go solely on the recommendation of a friend. The chemistry that your friend had may not be there between you and that same photographer. Research her photos so that you know and like her work. All photographers have their own style, but make sure their style doesn't overpower the subject matter – namely you.

Schedule an interview with the photographer before the shoot to make sure that you feel relaxed and comfortable with her. If you feel ill at ease, the photos will reflect that. Bring previous headshots as a starting-off point to discuss what you did and didn't like about them. Discuss archetypes and how you'd like to be cast. If you've been playing lots of doctors but would like to start broadening your range, devise ways to suggest that with subtle dress choices. If you have an agent or manager, make sure he participates in the discussion. You, the photographer and the agent should be working as a team to create your branding.

At the session itself, bring several different dress choices so you can aim for a range of looks within your archetypes. A good photographer will direct the session, but don't rely solely on the photographer's inspiration. It's your job to find motivations that turn the wheels in your head, and keeps your eyes engaged. You are the one in front of camera, so come prepared with ideas. Keep lines in your head from roles you have played, or that you want to play. Playing active objectives and making strong choices are effective in shoot sessions just as they are in auditions.

Above all, enjoy the session. If you're in pain, then so is your audience.

The more you relax and enjoy the session, the better the photos will be.

Choosing your headshot

There was a time when casting directors worked only from stacks of 8' x 10' photos. The computer age has changed this as we now view pictures as thumbnails on computers and two inch mobile phone screens. When I post a breakdown on Breakdown Services or Spotlight, I get thousands of suggestions and they appear on my computer screen in thumbnail size. I peruse them, choosing the more interesting and appropriate options to explore further. Sometimes when I Google an actor, all I can find is a tiny image that refuses to enlarge. So the moral of the story is, choose a photo that also works as a thumbnail.

The biggest mistake that actors make is choosing their own headshot; in those cases we nearly always end up with the most flattering image. The most beautiful shot is not necessarily the one that will get you the most work. Consult with your agent, the photographer, teachers, classmates and actor friends, before you make a decision. People who know you are at an advantage because they can tell if the picture 'captures' you and who you are. They are at a disadvantage because they are biased, and filter you through their own particular shade of lenses. The shot that your mother or boyfriend likes is not necessarily the shot that will book you the job.

People who don't know you have the advantage of being completely unbiased and may give you a more balanced opinion. There are actors' websites and forums where you can post your headshot and get feedback. Ask specific questions when eliciting feedback. 'What types of role do you see me playing?' or 'How would you cast me?' The opinionaters are unlikely to agree, so in the end it's your call. Choose a headshot that you are proud to hand over to casters.

It's one thing to photograph people. It is another to make others care about them by revealing the core of their humanness.
PAUL STRAND

Digital or hard copy?

Yes, it's true that in the casting business we are increasingly relying on digital images on the Internet. Fewer and fewer headshot prints pass through my hands. However, the good old 8' x 10' or A4 size is still necessary and in circulation. We use them for our casting boards. Always have a photo with you when you arrive at castings. Yes, your agent should have sent it, but don't rely entirely on him. Agents are fallible and casting directors lose things so take responsibility for putting it in our hands. It doesn't hurt to bring a digital copy as well on a USB stick.

Things to remember from this chapter

- The headshot is the first marketing tool a casting director sees.

- Make sure that it works in thumbnail size.

- Spin it to your market.

- Show us how you want to be cast.

- Choose your photographer carefully and enjoy your photo session.

15

CV or resumé[1]

Tell all the truth but tell it slant.

EMILY DICKINSON

Your resumé is not simply a list of all the work you've ever done. The Curriculum Vitae (CV) or resumé is a marketing tool edited to get you work. Never lie, but spin. Display the accurate and true facts in the order that will best present you for the roles for which you want to be considered. Some actors mistakenly think that to impress casters they should list as many projects as possible. On the contrary, this is a brilliant way to bury your true accomplishments in a sea of words. Help us by selecting your best and most relevant credits.

Make sure that all of the information on your resumé is very clearly presented and itemized. CVs are laid out slightly differently in the US and the UK. Lucinda Syson recounts a time when a US producer sat in on her casting session in London. All heads turned when the producer asked the actor if his hobbies were shopping and f**king. That's apparently what she thought it said on his CV. She didn't realize that *Shopping and F**king* is the name of a play by Mark Ravenhill.

Toss out rules that say you must list work strictly in chronological order and in an exactly uniform way each time. Feature your most

---

[1]These documents are called a CV in Europe and a Resumé in the US.

prominent work first. If your best leading role was last year, then put that project at the top, and list this year's project, in which you played the supporting role, below it. It's not a lie. It's spin.

A professional resumé is generally organized as follows:

- Name in **Bold** at the top, with contact or agent contact information.

- Include your accurate:
  - height (in appropriate measurements. Remember that Americans don't know the metric system and people who don't live on those islands off the coast of Europe don't know what a 'stone' is);
  - colour of hair and eyes;
  - playing range, not age;
  - Union Status: SAG (Screen Actors Guild) or Equity, etc. If you don't have membership, skip the section entirely. (Sometimes non-SAG members are preferred on independent projects.)

Trim the resumé to one page, itemizing 'selected credits' neatly in three, easy-to-read, columns. List your best area first. For example if you have a lot of strong stage credits, push them to the top. Otherwise list as follows:

- *Film.* List your best projects first. If your experience is limited, include student films and unpaid video work. Aside from naming the title of the project in the first column, there is no one right way to list your credits. In North America, actors often denote their billing in the second column. That means: Lead, Supporting, Featured, or Extra. Some actors list the name of the role, but that is less informative. Some actors simply list the project, the director and the company, without mentioning what they played in it. Make your decision based on what showcases you the best.

- For the third column, list the most impressive thing about the film. For example, mention the production company if it was produced by a big studio. If it was an unknown production company, but a well-respected director, like Gus Van Sant, then hustle his name into the column. If it was a small independent film produced by George Lucas' company, then George Lucas gets the third column place. If everything about the film was unknown, except the star, then go ahead and mention that it was 'starring Ben Kingsley' or whatever.

- *TV* comes after film, or can be listed under one heading, **'Film and TV'.** If you choose to list your billing, the standard is; Series Regular, Recurring, Guest Star or Co-Star. Your billing should be denoted in your contract, if you have any doubt.

- *Web series/Internet* is a legitimate category as well, and usually comes under TV.

- *Theatre.* If you're brand new on the scene, you can list school theatre. Everyone has to start somewhere. For theatre, the three columns are play, role, and the name of the theatre company and/or director (whichever is better.) If you played a lead in an unknown play, feel free to write 'Gary (lead)'.

- *Commercial/Industrial.* If you have a long list of commercial credits you may want to write, 'conflicts available upon request'. That way, the commercial credits don't overwhelm your CV, if you're working on developing a film career. Conflicts mean that when you've represented one brand of soap, you can't appear in a commercial for another brand of soap in the same year.

- *Training.* Here you can list a university degree, and any training courses or teachers with whom you're studying. If you're just starting out, and your strongest suit is your education, you can list it at the top if you wish. Casters like to see that your training is ongoing.

- *Special Skills:* Your skills and interests can be important in the casting process, but never lie. If you ride a horse, denote at what level (intermediate recreationally, professionally, etc.). If you sing, that means not only that you can carry a tune, but that you sing professionally. Mention your voice range (tenor, alto, etc.). Be sure that you can really do the accents you have listed properly. You may have to prove it at an audition. Mention if you speak a foreign language and at what level. Mention if you have a driver's licence.

In North America the resumé is stapled to the back of the photo. The other option is to include a thumbnail-sized headshot in the upper left corner of your CV (I prefer left corner, because the eye reads left to right) in addition to a contrasting photo on the back. It's essential that the photo and the resumé stay together.

Sample #1: Dufflyn Lammers' resumé

CV 1 is a sample resumé from actor Dufflyn Lammers. You can see that she has it neatly laid out in three columns so we can easily read it. Dufflyn is a working actor and has many more credits than she is listing but she simplifies it for the reader, making it scannable and drawing our eye to her best credits.

Sample #2: Novice CV

My agent, Jeremy Conway, provided this example (CV 2) of a young actor who he is representing. At time of print, Barnaby Sax only just graduated from Oxford School of Drama. So his CV is laid out a bit differently than it would be if he had been working for fifty years. They draw attention to his training at a very good conservatory.

∀ƃuǝ⅄ H∀ԀԀƎN ᴉɥⱢ

DUFFLYN LAMMERS SAG/AFTRA

http://speedreels.com/talent/dlammers/dlammers.html

FILM

RAVEN ****	Lead	Dir., Juan Azulay	Independent
BIRTHDAY SUIT *	Supporting	Dir., B. Cornelius	Independent
SPENT	Lead	Dir., Adam Blaker	Independent
PROUD AMERICAN	Supporting	Dir., Fred Ashman	Independent
ANGELA NOTHING	Lead	Dir., Juan Azulay	Independent
SURVIVAL OF THE FITTEST **	Supporting	Dir., Daria Price	Independent
LOOKING FOR MY BROTHER***	Supporting	Dir., Nathaniel McCullagh	Independent
BELLY	Supporting	Dir., Christmas Rini	ARTISAN
RULE NUMBER ONE	Supporting	Dir., David Presley	Independent
FIRE AND ICE	Supporting	Dir., Robert Burns	Independent

Sedona International Film Festival, Tallgrass, Real Dakota Film Festival 2011
** Worldfest, Houston, 2005 Remi Award Winner*
**Dances With Films Festival, 2005 Fusion Short Winner*
*** Action on Film International Film Festival, 2006 BEST PICTURE*
**** Los Angeles International Underground Film Festival, 2012, BEST EXPERIMENTAL*

TELEVISION

ENTOURAGE	Co-Star	Dir., Mark Mylod	HBO
CRIMINAL MINDS	Co Star	Dir., Steve Shill	CBS
RUSSEL SIMMONS DEF POETRY	Guest Star	Dir., Stan Lathan	HBO
MAD ATOMS	Guest Star	Dir., David Brooks	FOX Atomic

THEATER

WORD OF MOUTH	Principal	The Lee Strasberg Institute,
STOP KISS	Callie	City Lights Theatre

COMMERCIAL
Conflicts available upon request

TRAINING

Private (monologue)	Sam Christiansen	Sam Christiansen Studios
Private (improvisation)	Stephen Book	Stephen Book Studio
Private (on-camera)	Wendy Davis	L.A. Actors' Center
Private (scene study)	J D Lewis	The Actor's Lab
B.A. Liberal Arts	Paul Austin	Sarah Lawrence College, NY

SKILLS
L.A.P.D. Detective Training Unit. Spoken Word Poet. Young Storytellers Foundation Mentor. Authentic Southern Accent.

Charles Finlayson, THE HAPPEN AGENCY (818) 588-6437 www.thehappenagency.com

CV 1

Conway van Gelder Grant Ltd

8-12 Broadwick Street, London W1F 8HW   Tel: 020 7287 0077   Fax: 020 7287 1940

BARNABY SAX

Eyes: Dark brown   Hair: Brown   Height: 6'2   Training: Oxford School Of Drama

SKILLS
Banjo, Ukulele, Guitar, Mandolin, Piano

ACCENTS
London/RP (native), Heightened RP, Cockney, Glasgow, General American, New York, Southern American

THEATRE

LAUGHTON	Raymond/David/Terry	Stephen Joseph Theatre	Chris Monks
PRIDE & PREJUDICE	Wickham plus others	New Shakespeare Company	Deborah Bruce
ANTHONY & CLEOPATRA	Dolabella/Demetrius/ Soldier	Chichester Festival Theatre	Janet Suzman
TWO BEAN BAGS	Phoebe Waller-Bridge	Soho Theatre	Vicky Jones
SERIOUS MONEY	Eddie Durkfeld	Royal Court	Jessica Swale
TWELFTH NIGHT	Antonio	Oxfordshire Tour	George Peck

OXFORD SCHOOL OF DRAMA - THEATRE

The Relapse	Edward Loveless	Cordelia Monsey
Anna Karenina	Stiva	Hal Chambers
The Crucible	Paris	Juliet Seal

OXFORD SCHOOL OF DRAMA - FILM

Finding Home	Darren	Stefano Margaritelli
The 11th Commandment	Paul	Sirius Flatz

www.conwayvangeldergrant.com

Directors: Jeremy Conway, Nicola van Gelder, John Grant

CV 2

Things to remember from this chapter

- Don't lie, but spin your CV.
- Make it easy to read and scan.

16

Show reels and video clips

In your marketing campaign, think of the headshot and resumé as your print advertisement, and the reel as your commercial. For actors who wish to work on screen, it is imperative to create video material that a casting director can quickly and easily access. When we post breakdowns on Actors Access, Spotlight and other sites, we are presented with hundreds of options. If I come across an unknown actor who looks interesting, but who doesn't have a clip, I may move past her to another actor who shows me a sample of her work.

Show reel vs video clips

If you want to work on screen, video clips will be an important part of your marketing campaign.

In the previous version of this book, I recommended that actors hire a professional editor to cut their reel. I've slightly revised my thinking. It's great to have one professionally cut reel that you can post on IMDb, or use to target an agent. On the other hand, if you're working often, you don't want a reel that is so tightly edited that you can't freely and easily edit in new work yourself. At the Prague Film School, where I head the film acting programme, I make sure that all of our students learn editing. That way, they can continue to update their own reels as their work matures. Editing is not hard, and any laptop computer comes with some sort of basic editing program.

Clips

Frequently, actors are eliminating reels altogether, and just offering a selection of clips. The more successful actor websites will offer the viewer the choice of clips according to genre – comic, action clips, etc. You can also use specific clips to hone in on particular roles. Gary Marsh at Breakdown Services recommends, 'Submit a clip that matches the tone of the project you're submitting for. Don't give ten clips, give two and describe them.' This can be done in the naming of the clip itself. For example, if you are putting yourself up for a drama, you might send a clip called 'Clip from *Homeland*, playing opposite Damien Lewis.' Or if you are up for a forensic TV series, send a clip called, 'Procedural interview in NCIS.'

Castit Talent offers the opportunity for actors to promote themselves in 'packages'. Premium members can create a combination of headshots, resumé and video for specific genres. This allows actors to present a comedy package for sit-com roles, and a dramatic package for serious roles, and so on.

Reel

If you do decide to showcase a reel, realize that just as the resumé is not a list of all your projects, the reel is not a collection of everything you've ever done. It is a carefully edited selection of your best work. Your reel should be accessible 24/7 at the click of a button. That means posting it on YouTube and your website, making sure it will show up on search engines. If I Google your name and 'reel', I should be able to see it immediately – without a password. I don't understand when actors password-protect their reels. What's wrong with the whole world seeing your work? Hard copies of reels are less common now, but there does exist a very clever card for actors containing an imbedded reel, that flips out of the card, as a USB.

The image you present on the reel needs to match your primary headshot, so that's a good place to start. Begin the reel with a still of your headshot so we have no doubt whose reel we're watching.

Some actors start with a montage of different shots set to music to introduce themselves. I can tolerate a montage only if it is very short (for example, three different shots). Some editors choose to display a painfully long montage opening, full of fluff. Casting directors will get bored quickly if there is not substance on the reel. Just as the headshot should be current, so should the reel. You might have been great as a child actor, but showing your baby pictures will not get you cast today.

When Shakespeare said, 'Brevity is the soul of wit', he must have been thinking about show reels – the shorter, the better. Producers, and directors don't have time to watch hours of footage. If your reel is more than two or three minutes, it's almost guaranteed that it won't be watched until the end. Zachary Weintraub of Z Productions suggests that it's better to trim a reel short and 'leave them wanting more'. If a casting director's curiosity about the actor is completely satisfied by the reel, then he is less likely to call him in for an audition.

Many actors miss the opportunity to sell themselves with poorly produced reels. Top mistakes include reels that:

- run too long;

- contain too much of one project, or similar material;

- feature other actors more than the presented actor;

- contain the right material but the editing is slow.

Or conversely are over-edited with snippets that:

- are too short to get a sense that the actor can create a whole character;

- contain unprofessionally recorded theatre;

- have poor sound quality;

- don't include contact information.

Since you don't know how long the viewer will stay tuned, front end your best work. The same idea applies if you share scenes with prestigious actors; showcase these clips first because a star lends immediate legitimacy. If you can carry a scene with Tom Hanks, then you can be trusted. Cut right to the chase in each scene. The filmmaker who produced your material is telling a story. You're not. You are advertising your brand. Jump right into the middle of the scene, to the heat of the argument, or the moment of discovery, then quickly move on to your next brilliant moment. Just as a flashlight only works on the strength of its weakest battery, so does a reel; leave out scenes that are sub-par.

Just as variety, change and opposition are interesting in a performance, this is also the case with a reel. Professional editor Weintraub advises: 'Use variation in the order: long scene, short scene, fast scene, slow scene, etc. The reel should be entertaining.' The variety should extend to the types of scenes you choose. Intersperse comedy with tragedy, action with costume drama, etc. Remember that clips that are too short can also vitiate the effectiveness of your reel. I want to see at least a few scenes that are long enough to demonstrate that the actor has created a cogent character arch, with inner depth.

Avoid two-shots in which the other actor is featured much more than you. We may end up casting your co-star instead. If you have original footage, you can even play around with the editing, leaving the shot hanging on you, while the other actor's voice is off camera. Make friends with the editor of every project you work on. Maybe he will help you get those clips that ended up on the cutting room floor. Actor Winter Ave Zoli was completely cut out of a movie early in her career. Because she was friendly with the director, she was able to pull all of the scenes she played with Sean Connery and created one of her first reels.

Think carefully about which clips you choose. Your favourite scene may not reflect your best work. An agent or editor is a more impartial arbitrator. Consider not just how you've *been* cast, but how you *want* to be cast and spin your choices accordingly. When negotiating your deal with the editor, establish how many cuts he'll do within the agreed fee. Circulate the first cut to directors and professionals you trust for feedback before the final cut. At the end of the day, it's *you* who must be satisfied, so make sure that you feel proud to post the final product on your website.

If you're just starting out . . .

If you don't have a film career yet, then creating a reel can be a daunting task. How can you cleverly cut together scenes that don't exist yet? This first question you should ask yourself is, 'Am I ready to make a reel?' Make sure you've had some training before you set off. Everyone has to start somewhere. If you're not experienced on screen, then your first priority should be to gain experience.

Collect footage by volunteering to appear in student films at a local film school or University. You never know when you're working with the next Martin Scorsese, and most importantly you're getting experience in front of camera. The director might even be willing to cut a reel for you in exchange for your performance. There are always independent directors seeking actors on no or low budgets. Get connected to the circuits and networking sites that link blossoming actors and directors.

Beginning actors can also collect footage from screen acting classes. There are production companies that specialize in producing show reels. That means that they provide a set, lighting and sometimes coaching, to shoot professional quality scenes specifically designed for a reel. Ultimately, it is not the reel itself that is important, so much as some kind of quality taped material. One option is to invest the money that you would have used in producing a reel, and collaborate with other like-minded artists to produce a short film or local web series.

Things to remember from this chapter

- Video footage is imperative for screen actor marketing.
- Consider using clips rather than an edited reel.
- Keep your reel short and well edited.
- If you're inexperienced, volunteer at a film school to collect footage.

17

The self-taped audition

When I wrote the first version of this book, the self-taped audition (sometimes also called virtual auditioning or E-casting) was still something of a novelty. It was something that actors were mildly frightened of and in some cases, couldn't be bothered to do. In the six years since my first edition, the demand for self-taped auditions has increased exponentially. In the early days, self-taping happened when an actor could not be physically present to meet with the casting director or production. Casters gave the actor sides for a specific role, the actor points the camera at herself, tapes and sends the clip digitally to production. This kind of auditioning started to be widely accepted in the late noughties and now it is the norm. For almost any project that I cast, a substantial proportion of auditions will be self-generated outside of my studio. Sometimes self-tapes are used as a screening device even when casting director and actor are in the same location. It is simply more time-effective.

I was the first casting director to use Eco-Cast via Breakdown Services in 2010. I was casting a feature film called *Sniper Re-Loaded* and virtual casting allowed me to sit in my office in Prague and cast actors from Germany, England and Los Angeles to shoot on location in South Africa. Call-backs were a Skype call with director, Claudio Faeh in South Africa. At time of publishing an average of 4,000 virtual auditions pass through Eco-Cast every week. Castit in the US and E-TALENTA in Europe also provide platforms for actors to directly mail in self-taped clips to a casting director.

Self-tape auditions are both an exciting and daunting prospect. Thanks to the Internet, geography no longer prevents auditioning. At the same time, it puts more responsibility on the actor to learn the technology and techniques that were before only in the casting director's hands. Actors have to be ready and equipped to tape themselves at any moment. The actors who learn the skills and technologies to effectively self-tape will be the ones who work. Actors who cling to technophobia will be left behind. It's not just the most talented actor who gets the work. It is the most talented actor, who can get his work effectively and swiftly to production in time for them to make a decision.

Electronic auditioning has changed the way films and TV series are cast. It has allowed actors from much broader geographic regions to work. Whereas casting was once centralized in New York and Los Angeles, now actors can be cast from anywhere, any time. On *Mission Impossible IV*, I virtually cast an actor from Finland to shoot in Dubai, and an actor from Sarajevo to shoot in Vancouver. New York casting director, Mark Hirschfeld, cast Australian actor Luke Arnold as one of the leads in the Starz series *Black Sails* after he received a self-tape and then re-directed his second read via Skype. Beatrice Kruger cast Paris-based actor, Corrado Invernizzi from a self-audition he did in France for *Marco Polo* shooting in Italy. The examples are too numerous to mention. It's exciting to live in a true world market.

In a vast country like the United States, virtual casting has allowed actors from Dallas, Texas to book roles on projects shooting in Houston, more than three hours away. Actors from Seattle, Washington regularly virtually audition for series like *Legit, Grimm* and *Leverage* shooting in Portland, Oregon. Actors from the entire South East work on series such as *Homeland, Nashville* and *Eastbound and Down*.

Technology has opened up a lot of doors to regional casting directors. I can be having a very ho-hum session, but then I turn to the video submissions we've received, and there are OFTEN amazing talent who just weren't able to make the trek into town on that particular day. It makes it much more feasible for the actor who lives in, for example, Seattle to work on a project in Portland, when we're frequently casting directly from submitted videos. I'd estimate that 25% of our television bookings come from self-taped submissions. It basically opens my doors to many more talents than we previously had access to.

ERYN GOODMAN, regional casting director, Portland, Oregon. Works on *Grimm, Leverage, Legit*

So in the years since I started casting, I can say that virtual casting technique has definitely improved but we still get submissions from talented actors that are unfortunately so poorly done that we can't pass them on to the director. It doesn't matter how great your performance is if we can't see your eyes or hear you. Shaky camera work and shabby backgrounds can similarly cheapen a good performance.

Self-tape casting services

There are a number of services that cater to virtual auditioning, and more are springing up every day. There are even organic businesses that have sprouted up in actors' homes to accommodate this new way of casting. Look online in your community to see what the buzz is.

Some agencies have also set up casting rooms at their headquarters and will help actors self-tape.

The major online services that casting directors engage are:

- *Eco-Cast* (http://breakdownexpress.com/content/ecocast. html) which is a virtual auditioning service, at Breakdown Services. Eco-Cast enables a casting director to easily distribute sides to actors who self-tape and then upload their audition to a central location where production can view all auditions in one place.

- *Castit* (castittalent.com) is another major company in Los Angeles that many of the big studios use to view audition clips. It was originally designed by CEO Chris Gantos as a tool for casting directors to easily access their casting lists from current and previous projects and have video instantly available to show directors and executives during a casting brainstorm session. Castit has hardware that allows casting directors to easily invite actors to self-tape and upload to a central site. For actors, Castit developed Castittalent.com where its Open Call section is continually posted for actors to submit directly to productions.

- *E-TALENTA* is the prime European site that Italian casting director, Beatrice Kruger, has worked tirelessly to create. E-TALENTA is accessible in six languages and features free and advanced (paid) memberships for actors. Actors can create profiles with reels, photos and resumés and send them to casters instantly, thus eliminating heavy email files. It enables agents to promote talent at the click of a button, and also hosts self-tape casting features and breakdowns released by casting directors.

- *Spotlight*. At time of publication, Spotlight in London was developing self-tape technology. Check their website.

It's important to know how to prepare an effective audition. It might sound like a piece of cake, but many actors find it hard to set up the taping themselves. As a former technophobe, I can assure you there's nothing complicated about operating a basic video camera. Learn it and consider it one of the skills that an actor should know to succeed in today's film world. The disadvantage of taping yourself is that you don't have the benefit of a director. The advantage is that you can prepare the session in the comfort of your own home, and practice with multiple takes. So take a breath, relax and here are some guidelines.

Steps in self-taped auditioning

Equipment

1 *Camera.* Every actor should have her own camera. Video cameras are affordable and useful. High-end, high-tech equipment is not necessary. Invest a few hundred dollars for an amateur camera.

2 *Can you use a smart phone?* Yes, but only in a pinch. I have successfully cast actors from iPhone auditions. Very important make sure you turn it landscape, not portrait. The portrait images have a way of flipping upside down when they are delivered.

3   *Tripod.* The image should be stable. This is why I say that the smart phone can work but only in a pinch. I have seen too many shaky camera auditions. Position the tripod so that it shoots straight across to you. Don't shoot up or down on yourself unless you are trying to create a specific effect.

4   *Miscellaneous equipment.* A secondary investment might be a separate microphone, as internal microphones are often poor. Inexpensive mics are available at camera stores. An external mic will take care of the problem we often experience of hearing the off-screen reader (who is next to the lens) louder than the actor. Gary Marsh from Breakdown Services suggests buying cheap cone lamps from home supply stores, and mounting them on a ladder. Overhead lighting is not the best as it can make the eyes look sunken. The most important thing is that your eyes are well lit. There is a website called Filmtools.com that you can use to order film equipment.

5   Find *a solid neutral background* in your home, a plain wall or curtain. Avoid shooting in front of a window, patterned wall paper, or busy bookshelves. Create a space that looks like a studio even if it really is your bedroom.

Preparation

Once you get hold of the scene, follow the steps already outlined in this book. First you want to answer the basic acting questions:

- Who am I?
- Where am I?
- Who am I talking to?
- What do I want?
- What are the stakes?
- Where are the changes/discoveries?

Shooting

There is no formula for shooting the perfect virtual audition. The most important thing is to follow the specific instructions of the production. Sometimes they will want you to introduce yourself in a certain way, or shoot yourself in wide frame, or close up. For the *Spartacus* audition, we needed all actors to audition bare-chested, for example, but that would be totally weird in another context!

If a casting director sends you sides without instructions, then the only rule is to present yourself well. Make sure the lighting is good, the camera is straight. I appreciate a short introduction announcing the role you are reading for. I have definitely seen actors introduce themselves for far too long. I also recommend showing both wide and close shots of yourself, so that we can get an idea of what you look like. You can do this by having your camera operator start with a wide shot, then gradually zooming in. Or if you don't have a camera operator, you can choose to show yourself wide in the introduction and closer in the audition, for example.

If you're reading with a scene partner (could be the camera operator), place them directly at eye level behind the camera lens. If you prefer to find a focus point, rather than reading with a person, choose a spot near the camera lens, so that we can see you. Looking next to the lens (rather than into it) will give us a good three-quarters view of your face.

Play variety and range. If you do two takes, make each take different. There is no point in sending two versions, unless there is new information the second time around.

Make sure you're listening (see Chapter 11 on listening). Remember that a large proportion of film acting is listening and not speaking. Don't throw away your best acting moments that happen during the silences. Avoid acting without a partner, unless it's a monologue. It's important to have a partner (even a non-actor) to read the other lines. I've even seen actors who recorded their own voices in the other lines.

Sending the audition clip

There is only one right way to do it; the way the casting director or production tells you to. If they ask for the clip to be a certain size or compression; then you must do it exactly as they ask or it may not fit into their viewing format. In some cases the material is even loaded into an HD converter so that the director can view it on HD. I often ask for material to be sent very small, for example, less than 20MB. When it's big, it looks better but in some cases I ask actors to compromise quality so that I can quickly load it.

Unless specifically requested, avoid using sites like YouTube for auditions. Even if it is password-protected, you might find that your auditions are public material some day.

What not to do

I'll give you the opportunity to learn from some bad examples I've seen.

Don't try to shoot a professional film

Some actors mistakenly think that they must produce a mini-film and go out of their way to acquire costumes, sets and professional editing. ('You should watch my tape for the locations alone,' one actor said to me. Indeed, that was the best part!) One actor who was auditioning to play a taxi driver decided he needed to tape in a car. I couldn't understand a word he was saying as the engine was so loud. Remember that the casting tape should be as simple as possible. You want the director to be looking at you and your raw acting ability, not your sets and costume design skills.

Do not include a scene partner in the shot

Not unless you want them to be cast too. The person you're reading with should be off camera. If they're a good actor, that's fine, but it's not a necessity. You risk that the director will become more interested in the other players than you. (I've seen it happen. 'He's not so good but what about *her*?')

Don't worry about complicated blocking

Remember the KISS rule (Keep It Simple, Stupid). There are all kinds of creative ways that a director may choose to shoot a scene. This does not apply to auditions. Shoot yourself from the most flattering angle, but don't worry about shooting it creatively. Stick to the boring formula as described above; we'll see three-quarters of your face, aimed to a point near the lens most of the time.

Don't throw away the best moments in the scene

Remember that so much of acting is in reacting. Sometimes it is the moments in between the text, the reaction shots, that reveals the character's inner feelings. I've seen too many audition clips in which actors concentrate on speaking the lines rather than on reacting.

Self-casting: do's and don'ts

Do	Don't
Introduce yourself briefly, saying your name, height and agent.	Announce your age, unless it is specifically requested.
Keep your shots simple. Face the camera and expose at least three-quarters of your face most of the time.	Get fancy with editing or shooting.
Have your scene partner read off screen and close to the camera lens. The camera should always be on you.	Focus the camera on any actor other than yourself. Unless you want to audition your scene partner as well.
Use a simple background.	Shoot on a location, use elaborate sets, costumes and props.
Sit close to the microphone, or get a professional separate microphone.	Stand far from the microphone, so that your scene partner is louder on the tape then you are.
Practise with several takes, but just choose a few.	Send in many takes.

Mount the camera on a tripod so the shot is steady.	Hand-hold the camera, unless you have a very steady hand.
Make sure your eyes are well lit.	Sit with the window behind you.
Use a smart phone but only in a pinch. Invest in a decent video camera.	Shoot 'portrait' on a smart phone.

18

Internet casting
and online presence

Where do you go when you want to buy or find something? You go to the Internet of course. So where do you think casting directors go when they're looking for actors? Today in casting everything happens fast, fast, fast and online. Agents submit actors electronically to casting directors, who receive hundreds of submissions in the first hour after a breakdown is posted. Almost the moment an actor auditions for me, I pop her onto file-share for the producers and director.

In the 1990s when cell phones were newly popular, I remember an actor's comment that, 'Having a cell phone is the difference between getting the job or not.' Indeed, then as now, casting is sometimes simply about getting an actor *quickly* to set. Having a cell phone now is a given, so the 'difference between getting the job or not' has to do with Internet presence. When I'm in an idea-storming session with a director, I may refer to an actor off the top of my head. If I can immediately access that actor's reel on the Internet, he's that much closer to the job. Producer Fred Roos marvels that 'The Internet allows access instantly to any actor who comes into your brain at the click of a button.' When the director has access to all of your materials online, he's more likely to shortlist you for the role, quicker than the actor without the web presence. Yes, it is your agent's job to market you, but getting your own materials online makes it much easier for your agent to sell you. You're giving her the tools she needs to help you book the job.

I suggest a four-pronged strategy for Internet presence:

1 Register on the major quality casting sites, and search engines.

2 Construct and maintain a website that uniquely markets you.

3 Be Google-able and YouTube-able.

4 Make use of social media.

While writing this chapter, I was teaching master classes in Istanbul, Turkey, during a politically tumultuous time in which the prime minister had shut down Twitter and YouTube. I was also casting a project and a few actors sent me their reels via YouTube. The lesson is to make sure that your promotional material is available on a variety of platforms (YouTube AND Vimeo AND speedreels, for example). You never know when a certain platform will be kaput for either political, technical (or who knows what?) reasons.

Casting sites and search engines

The Internet offers an indeterminable range of search engines designed for actors and the entertainment business. Although I list some of the major ones here, there are hundreds more, and by the time this book goes into print there will be new ones and the old ones will have new options and functions, so actors need to keep up with the ever-changing world.

Following is a list of major actor casting search engines, where smart actors maintain an active presence. There are many more sites that you can research and use at your discretion:

International

- IMDbPro (this is still developing, see Chapter 20 on IMDb)
- Let It Cast
- Casting Networks

USA and Canada

- Actors Access
- Now Casting
- Casting About
- Casting Notebook
- Castit
- LACasting
- Backstage Casting

UK

- Spotlight
- Casting Call Pro
- Cast Web
- Shooting People (for independent projects in the US + UK)

Europe

- E-TALENTA (in six languages)

Australia

- Showcast.com.au

The website

The actor search engines are essential but they are not enough. There are directors who aren't using those sites, or who are looking outside the box. I believe that a website, properly designed, is a worthwhile investment. If money is tight, I have seen actors successfully design their own websites. It is not expensive to buy your own domain, such as *www.wendywannarole.com*. This enables you to devise a professional email address as well such as wendy@wendywannarole. com. A website enables you to brand and market yourself in a unique way because you can control the content and presentation. In any campaign, the marketers will ask the following three questions first:

1   What do you do?

2   Who are your customers?

3   Why should they buy from you?

Let these marketing questions guide the content of your website.

- *What do you do?* Make it clear that you're a professional actor. Don't muddle the site with too many conflicting images or extracurricular interests that could lead viewers to think that acting is a hobby. If you are expert in something else that enhances your acting, such as stunts, horseback riding, stand-up comedy or dance, then devote some space to it. But make sure it's not too prominent or it will look like you're a stuntman or dancer before an actor.

- *Who are your customers?* Harrison Ford knows that he's a product. In a radio interview he referred to 'the audience' as his 'customer'. According to talent manager Derek Power, 'You have to create a billboard for yourself. You have to market yourself. You are your own product. That means you should have a website. Treat yourself as a business with one client that has to be branded, and merchandised to an audience who are casting directors, producers, directors. Ultimately they are your customers.' Figure out what information they would need to cast you. Ensure your site's usability for all customers by testing it on the different browsers, products and programs in use like Mac and PC, Firefox and Outlook. One time I couldn't access an actor's reel on my Mac computer. Because I was very interested in her, I switched to my PC and found success, but she would have been out of the race if I had been either marginally interested, or without both types of computers.

> Working in Hollywood does give one a certain expertise in the field of prostitution.
>
> JANE FONDA

- *Why should they buy from you?* Good question. There are millions of actors in the world. So what makes you special? Why should they cast you? In other words, what is the product? What are you selling? We have established that you are selling yourself. That makes it sound like prostitution, doesn't it? No wonder there is a historic connection between acting and prostitution. But no, that's not quite it. You're selling your image and your range of abilities as an actor. What makes you special as an actor? Identify your image and the range of archetypes that you play. Through your own personal style you will reflect, on the site, what you have to offer, how you look, what your experience is, how you've trained. 'All things spring from the client's identity,' claims web designer Deborah Dewitt, 'which incorporates, logo, logotype, fonts, colors, graphics, photos and layout – all of these combine to visually represent their offering, personality and communication style.' This design style can tie in with the design on your reel, and all of your presentation materials. The site expresses the predominant archetypes that you play.

> Developing a site which reflects the individual's strengths and style is critical in having a website that stands out from the crowd. Are the roles the actor books the police officer, the CEO or the down on his/her luck, struggling single parent? The website should reflect the personal style of the actor so there is no doubt in the casting director's mind, 'Yes, I can use this person for my comedy!'
> ELLEN TREANOR STRASMAN, founder of Actors Webmaster

An effective actor's website will include the following: a clear home page and an efficient drop-down menu.

> Two items are paramount in web designs: clarity and navigation. Your identity and message should be quickly and easily recognized within the first few seconds that someone lands on your homepage. If it isn't, most people will quickly navigate away to another site or search engine.
>
> DEB WILSON, DSW Design

The home page will prominently feature the actor's one main headshot. It's best not to clutter it with tons of different images. Save multiple photos for the gallery. Google likes changing content, so announce news, like a new show, or snippets of good reviews on the front page. You might prefer to vlog info in video format rather than to write it. Not only will it keep us up to date but it will make your site easier for search engines to find. You will also decide on this page what your menu items will be.

The menu items should include the following:

- *Resumé*. Here you may decide to organize your resumé with selected credits as described earlier, or PDF of full credits for download. Some actors skip the resumé and link into a search engine, such as Breakdown Services or IMDb for their resumé. This is handy because then they don't have to worry about updating two sites, but I would recommend posting your resumé separately on the site as well. Provide downloadable and printable options to make it easier for casting directors to obtain hard copies. Make sure your contact info is on the printable copies.

- *Biography*. This optional heading is a short prose section that includes where you were born, and how you've got where you are. It is a way to emphasize your background, and what makes you unique. If you escaped from war-torn Yugoslavia, for example, that could inform your experience for a given role. If you grew up in the suburbs of New York, or Kent, it could be equally as relevant, depending on the project. The style in which the biography is written also provides an opportunity to express your personality and sense of humour.

- *Gallery*. Here's a chance to show the range of archetypes you can play and to offer additional information about yourself. The headshot is limited, as it is usually just that – the head. Take this opportunity to show a wider shot, so we can see your wonderfully round, or modestly slim frame. If your main headshot is quite serious, but you're also good at comedy, then include a photo that reflects this side of you. If you mostly play contemporary but are also a Shakespearean trained actor, post production stills with period costume. Be selective about what images you choose, however. Web expert Ellen Treanor Strasman notes that one of the frequently made mistakes is when, 'Actors choose to put in too many photos. The average visit time per page is less than one minute so people won't look at that many photos. The rule of lists is (and this applies to the number of photos) people will look at the first three and the last one.' So put the strongest photos in these four positions.

In this early draft of a website gallery by Russian actor Alexandra Callas, she made the mistake of crowding too many images that look too much alike. In the first several images, she doesn't share with us any new information. If you look at her current website, you will see that she has corrected it.

GALLERY 1
Photographers: Stanislav Callas, Olga Fomina and Katya Kerbel

In the next gallery, my former Prague Film School student, New York actor Brian Colin Foley displays an easy-to-read format of photos. There aren't too many, and in the three neat columns, we can easily absorb the information and different archetypes he displays.

GALLERY 2
Photographers: Sam Haddix, Taylor Hooper and Dafna Ljubotina

- *Reel.* Don't miss this part. When I'm considering an actor I don't know, I always watch their reel. There is no substitute for the moving picture. Some actors separate their work by project, showing a few clips from each. Other actors divide their clips up by type – for example, comedy, drama, action – and make mini reels. Usually actors load up their two- or three-minute reel. Make sure that the links work and are in a common format that viewers can watch, like QuickTime. The reel and each clip should start with your image so we're not confused about who we should be watching. If you have clips in different language, separate them.

- *Press or reviews* (optional). This section will include snippets of reviews about you. You can link to the whole article, or quote one or two sentences. If you got a good notice within a bad review, feel free to pick out the phrase that flatters your performance.

- *Contact.* If you have an agent, include all of their contact details. Many casters prefer the professional distance that an agent affords. If you don't have an agent, or don't mind being contacted directly, an auto-form is a way of concealing your personal email address.

Other sections that you might include are:

- *Voice over.* If you do voice work, and have a voice reel, include that.

- *Links.* Links to and from the site are important for drawing viewers. Link your page to a professional search engine, your agency or link to a project you're working on, and ask them to link back to you. The more links there are *to* your site, the more traffic you'll get, which will push your site to the top of the search engines.

Top three mistakes made on websites:

1 Using a fancy introduction.

2 Muddling your message with too many conflicting images. Know who you are, and choose only relevant images.

3 Neglecting to keep your page up to date.

The most common mistake is thinking that a site using Flash with all kinds of moving elements will be great. The fact is most people hit the 'skip intro' button and the bottom line is, content is king. Plus visitors to the site want to control their experience and Flash does not allow people to do that, it is more passive. It also hurts your chances with search engines like Google since Flash programs can't be read or cataloged.

ELLEN TREANOR STRASMAN, Actors Webmaster

Suggestions from web designer, Deborah Dewitt of DSW Design

You must present a compelling visual story that meets the visitor's needs in a user-friendly format that is fast and simple to digest.

Design examples

1 Collect logos and type styles that you like. Don't worry if they aren't related to acting or the film industry.

2 Pull out magazine ads that strike you. Illustrations, photography and artwork are also good resources.

3 Paint stores are a great place to look at colours. Grab your favourites in convenient sample strips.

4 Bookmark web sites that capture your attention, for either design or navigational organization.

5 Pull together examples of any designs that resonate with you: books, CD/album jackets, product packaging.

6 Learn about yourself in this process. Are you logical and streamlined – your taste leaning toward clean, and striking designs? Or do you delight in fun, vibrant designs? Anything that captures your attention can be used for inspiration.

Identity considerations

- Your logo, stationery and marketing materials all carry both character and message to your audience. It's essential that your identity represents your business creatively, consistently and enduringly.

- *Creativity:* Your visual communications should be attractive, informative and compelling.

- *Consistency*: A consistently presented identity allows for recognition and retention by customers.

- *Endurance*: Your identity has to stand the test of time, avoiding trends or clichés.

19

Social media

Use of social media should be part of your marketing strategy. Once you have created the logo for your campaign – that is your headshot – make sure that it matches across all platforms. The image that you present on your website should match the image that you use on LinkedIn, Facebook, IMDb and Twitter.

In today's world, maintaining an online presence means being *active*, but more importantly ***interactive*** in social media. Are actors getting jobs and making connections via social media? The answer is, yes, they are. When I sent out a Facebook post asking actors to share their examples of how they booked jobs from social media, it was like trying to take a sip of water from a fire hose. There were so many examples that I can hardly enumerate them here.

Some people are allergic to social media, finding it privacy threatening, time consuming or intimidating. There are concerns that information collected on social media targets us via insidious advertising campaigns. The truth is that social media is changing advertising. Yes, companies will try to sell us products based on our likes and dislikes. We can cry about this or accept it. Moreover, as marketers we can use this to our own advantage. If you're an actor, you're a marketer and you need to be in the marketplace. Your goal is to create profiles that will let your buyers (casting directors, producers, etc.) come to you. Coordinate your efforts with your agent or manager, if you have one. Talent representatives often register concern if you can be contacted about work directly via social media so it's good to be on the same page about how you present yourself.

Use social media (Facebook, Twitter, YouTube, LinkedIn), because you're selling and that is where everyone is buying. Do you have to use *all* of these platforms? No, but please choose at least one social media site to lead casting directors, producers, directors TO you. How do you do this? By creating value and curiosity. Present yourself as a professional peer to the people with whom you want to connect. Nurturing these relationships will take time and patience until they come to fruition, so don't expect instant results.

Consider the most effective way to develop these relationships. In social media marketing there is something called the 80/20 rule. Post 80% interesting, inspiring, useful content that contributes to your community and reserve 20% for promotion of your own brand. If the 80% that you present is engaging, then you will develop followers who will actually pay attention when you exercise your 20% self-promotion rights.

Imagine that social media is like a big party. There is nothing more boring than hearing an actor (or anyone) rant on about how great they are, what they are doing, etc. Everyone has experienced that braggart who traps you in the corner and just doesn't stop talking about himself. Be the memorable guest at the party who is listening to others speak, supporting them and occasionally interjecting her thoughts and ideas. Your Facebook friends, LinkedIn contacts and Twitter followers are your community and you are all there to help and support one another. Read and reply to other people's posts, as well as your own. Isn't this just what your mother taught you – to be cooperative and supportive towards others? It's common sense. Be a *human being*, not just an actor.

To learn more about social media marketing, I highly recommend the research of Amy Jo Bermen, former casting director at HBO. She teaches classes and webinars for actors on social media marketing. Her example is that if you're at a party and Steven Spielberg is there, you don't want to run up to him and shove your headshot into his hands. You want to engage with him, on a peer level. Once he gets to know you a bit, and realizes how interesting you are, he'll come to you with a job. This is how social media works. 'Lead with value,' emphasizes Bermen.

At a film festival I once attended, casting directors were set up with actors on 'speed dates'. Some actors were nervous and spent the time trying to sell themselves. Other actors just sat and chatted. At the end of the day, I realized that the actor who I remembered the best was a Finnish actor, Jaspar Paakkonen, who spent the entire time chatting with me about his off-screen interest – fly-fishing. A relaxed conversation had led us there. Although I'm not a fisher myself, I became fascinated with his passion about the sport and his activism in saving fish populations. He was simply being a real person rather than working so hard to impress us. Other actors who I've remembered well were people who connected with me on a personal level. We had something in common, or shared a point of reference; we were building a peer relationship. It's not possible to build a meaningful relationship with everyone you meet, but only a few quality relationships are necessary.

The idea is that you want to draw people TO you, not repel them. I've observed this in my own interactions with actors. I meet thousands of actors at casting calls, festivals and master classes. The honest truth is that I can't remember them all, but there are certain ones who manage to stay in touch with me in a friendly and unobtrusive way. These are the actors who come to mind when a role comes up for them. There are others who are forever in touch but in an obnoxious way ... constantly spamming me, or writing long emails with too many questions that I can't take the time from my day to answer.

In my previous book, I recommended that actors send occasional newsletters to mailing lists, but I herewith revise this advice. People don't read newsletters unless they have requested them. I ignore most of the newsletters I get. When I log onto my Facebook page, however, I do so voluntarily. Social media is the way forward.

Goals on social media

1   Your first goal is to create and optimize your professional brand image as an actor. That means synching your logo/ headshot on all of your sites – Twitter, FaceBook, IMDb. All of these accounts will direct traffic to your website.

2   Your second goal is to build industry relationships. Many casting directors have professional Facebook pages and Twitter feeds. Once you join, do a hash tag or keyword search using words like Casting, Actor, Production, etc. to identify groups you want to join or individuals you want to follow.

3   Your third goal is to find opportunities for auditions, and events that you might not hear about via other channels. Other actors might even be your best source for these.

4   Stay informed. Join Twitter feeds from *Hollywood Reporter*, IMDb, Actors Access and *Variety*. Find out what's happening in your area, what the recent trends are, who is up and coming in the industry etc.

5   Help and inspire other people. Think of social media as a community of artists and pass useful information on to others. Perhaps you see a great opportunity for someone else. Pass it on. Help casting directors find someone even if the post is not right for you. That casting director will remember you next time. Promote actor friends and they will promote you when your time comes up.

See the following examples from my former student, Sarah Marie Brown. You see that she has presented a clear, simple, uncluttered image on the homepage of her website.

FIGURE 1
Photographer: Andrew Tester

FIGURE 2
Photographer: Andrew Tester

FIGURE 3
Photographer: Andrew Tester

FIGURE 4
Photographer: Andrew Tester

She has matched the headshot also on her Facebook, LinkedIn, Twitter and IMDb pages as well, thus effectively branding herself. Each time we see her, we are reminded of her brand.

Facebook

Facebook is more than one billion strong and growing. If used carefully, it can enhance your career and enrich valuable contacts. Make sure that your postings are few (averaging less than one per day) and of quality. If you post too many meaningless items in one day, your friends will eventually block or drop you. You may decide to separate your personal from your professional pages. Pay attention to your privacy settings, but bear in mind that privacy settings often change on Facebook and there is no guarantee that your 'private' photos won't be exposed. A good rule of thumb is as my friend Bonnie Gillespie (author of *Self-Management for Actors*) says, don't post anything on Facebook that you wouldn't want on the front page of the *New York Times*. Make sure that you manage your image. Don't let friends tag you unless you can approve the tag before it goes live. There is a good place for those drunk stag-night photos . . . but it's not on Facebook.

Fan page

A fan page could be premature if you're not famous yet. Some well-known actors find that their fans start the page before they do. Once this happens, you may decide to create an 'official fan page' that you can manage yourself. If you're not famous but in the stage of building your career, keep Amy Jo Bermen's advice in mind. You want to build relationships not fans.

Networking with casting directors

Facebook happens to be my personal social media of choice and, yes, I have cast actors from it, and stayed in touch with actors using Facebook. Many, but not all casters use it. I have a professional Facebook page which I keep separate from my personal page. My own rule of thumb is that my 'friends' are actors who I've met personally, so I don't accept requests from everyone. My professional page is where I share information, tips, promote my classes and ask questions to the professional world.

When you 'friend' or 'like' a casting director's page, don't expect instant results. Relationships take time to develop. Recently an actor joined my Nancy Bishop Casting page and rather abruptly messaged me asking 'OK I joined your page, where are the casting announcements?' This is an actor who doesn't understand social media. The trick is to build relationships and stay in a contact's peripheral vision. There are casting directors who post breakdowns but not all do. I do use Facebook for casting calls, but usually only if I'm looking outside of the box. For example, one time I needed a Middle Eastern actor, and one of my former workshop actors came forward on Facebook and reminded me that he was within driving distance of the shoot. He did end up getting the role. I can enumerate many examples like this. Most often these casting connections work well when local cast is needed. An actor should keep a list of the shooting locations where she has a place to stay and connect with casting directors in those regions (more about this in Chapter 26 on regional casting). Even if a casting director does not share breakdowns, she may provide useful tips, and help actors to stay in the loop, so it won't be a waste of time to make the connection.

> Use original photos when posting to social media sites. A picture always draws more attention than just words.

Twitter

Twitter can be enormously useful for contacting people with whom you may not otherwise be able to speak. For example, Grant Podelco, an actor I cast in an ABC series, tweeted the star player after his day on set, saying 'Very nice shooting today with Ashley Judd.' Ashley immediately tweeted back saying that it was nice to meet him as well. If he had asked for her phone number on set, do you think he would have got it? This was a way for him to make contact with her without any gatekeepers. Many production executives and stars even manage their own accounts. It's a way for them to stay in touch directly with their fans, and stay in the loop about what's being said about them. Many actors have reported to me that they have made contact with producers, writers and actors on Twitter where some people find it easier to break the ice.

LinkedIn

I originally joined LinkedIn in order to contact a certain person. It was the only way. It seems to be something that business people use more than 'artistic' people, but nevertheless, I did discover a new world of contacts this way. It was just simply too much for me to keep up with alongside Facebook and my website and emails, etc. So in my own personal case, LinkedIn maxed me out. So I'm lucky enough to have someone managing it for me. On LinkedIn, one can create groups, join active groups, ask for professional recommendations for your profile, and reciprocate skill endorsements. You can also connect with casting directors and agents. Reserve contacting them with a specific message for an important time when you have something concrete to ask – something more substantial than 'Please cast me in something.'

YouTube or Vimeo

Consider developing your own YouTube or Vimeo channel where you can put clips, demo reels, vlogs and other work. I encourage my students to develop their own web series.

How to ruin your career on social media

We all know and have heard stories about the downside of social media. There is no question that a wrong turn can damage your career. Please avoid the following pitfalls:

- *Drunk tweeting*: Be sure to avoid any kind of instant posting when you are angry, inebriated or in any kind of altered state. This is when mistakes are made and we send that message, instantly blasting our discontent to the universe; this could ruin us.

- *Divulging information about production, stars, casting*: There has been discussion in Hollywood about contractually forbidding actors from posting info about projects on social media sites while they are in production. Producers get very nervous about leaking information especially when secret plot twists are at stake. Don't be the actor who leaks information, starts rumours or outs gossip about co-stars.

- *No boasting*: Regarding your own work, I would advise you not to boast about booking a role until the contract is signed and you are on your way back from shooting. Sadly, things can change abruptly. Actors also have got in trouble for making it sound like they booked the role when they haven't yet; this angers production and never reflects well on the actor.

- *Spamming*: Once you do start to build relationships with industry professionals, be careful about how you interact with them. Constantly posting your show reel link on someone's page is not a way to meaningfully interact with them; it's spam. Make sure that your material has been requested before you send it.

Things to remember from this chapter

- Use of Social Media should be an integral part of an actor's campaign.

- You don't have to use all social media platforms, but choose at least one.

- Be not only active but interactive, helping others in your community as well as promoting yourself.

- Persistent use of social media can boost your career but it takes time to develop.

20

IMDb:

We love it, we hate it

What is IMDb?

It's IMDb's mission to be the top source for movie, TV and celebrity information. The Internet Movie Database is the largest known online record and rating system for films, TV programmes, video products and games, with complete listings of cast and crew, a kind of Wikipedia for both film industry professionals and layman alike. The site is one of the 50 most popular websites in the world, with 160 million monthly users.

The Internet Movie Database started as a passion project by a cinephilic, Hewlett Packard employee who just wanted to share and document his encyclopaedic knowledge of films. Col Needham (living in the provincial town of Stoke-Gifford in England – no Hollywood insider) had no idea that it was the beginning of a multi-million dollar business when he innocently started compiling and posting lists of data in 1989. When you cross a film geek with a computer nerd – the result is IMDb. He simply loves movies and has (at the time of press) watched and rated 8,524 of them.

Why is IMDb so important?

Not only did fellow cinephiles find this data delightful, but eventually the database caught on with industry professionals who now use it as a bible of information. From my own point of view it's infinitely helpful for any casting director in a brainstorming session with a director. 'What's the name of that actor who is in X film?' It's so easy to look things up. I even use it to check my own credits when I can't remember something! Casters, producers, directors are using IMDb every day to find and check credits on actors. Right or wrong, good or bad, your credits on IMDb legitimize you.

Should it be so important?

To be honest, while I do constantly use IMDb myself to check not only actors – but also the credits of producers or directors I might be working with – all the same I believe IMDb has become too powerful. You're nobody if you're not on IMDb. This isn't fair for many reasons. There are, for example, valuable film professionals who don't appear because they are working at the executive level where they are not necessarily credited on the print of a film (which is the ultimate blueprint from which IMDb works).

The other important job that entirely escapes its notice is foreign dubbing. It is not just any old actor who is allowed to dub a lead character in a top-rated film, but IMDb does not recognize this. If you have done this type of work, you might be able to slip it into the trivia section on IMDb Pro. Accomplished theatre actors also have no place on the site.

What actors need to know about IMDb

Although the site was sold to Amazon in 1998, it is still not 100% professionally manned with data entry personnel. It functions somewhat like Wikipedia which means it relies on the help of thousands of contributors to enter, correct and update information. These contributors may range from Star Trekkies to heads of studios. Is the data consistently reliable? No, it's not.

Consequently those of us who work in the biz must very consistently update our own information on IMDb, making sure that it is current and accurate. The best way to make friends with IMDb is to consistently contribute with accurate, and verifiable information. Once the site knows you as a reliable source, it will likely accept your updates with less difficulty. According to an unverifiable source, 70% of the IMDb staff are dedicated to the task of approving information that others post. Become a conscientious contributor to IMDb. Read the contributors' charter. Some people, like my producer friend, don't mind updating and correcting other people's information. When he sees an error on a film he's worked on, he'll correct it. The more one updates data in this way, the more the system will like this contributor.

I personally, on the other hand, am wary of updating other people's information because it could become a full-time obsession. While working on *Child 44*, I happened to check the IMDb page before the film had screened. The cast list was almost entirely wrong and reflected a *suggested* early cast. This gave me the spooks because I wondered how the database got this wrong information. Was some production assistant looking over my shoulder or did an IMDb spy pop his head in my office while we were in the process of casting? I almost screamed when I saw this false information but knew that it would be corrected once the print of the film was released, as per official IMDb policy. I have settled on a policy that I won't make actors' credits my responsibility. I advise actors and agents to take control of this process themselves on IMDb. If you're having trouble with them accepting your credit, you can take a screen-captured image or video of the credit appearing on screen and send it in with your request.

Use all of the resources available to you on IMDb. That means buying an IMDbPro account. Yes, it costs money, but if you are serious, you will invest in your career. With a Pro account, you can add a show reel, resumé, and take better control of what images are presented of you. You can write a bio and add trivia, etc. Be careful because once you post a bio, it can be expanded upon, but it is not easy to delete.

Using IMDb proactively

IMDb is encouraging casting directors to use the site to actually post breakdowns so that actors and agents can submit directly via the database. At time of print, I have been offered a free IMDbPro account as an automatic perk for CSA members. IMDb is in direct contact with the CSA coordinator trying to organize IMDbPro in such a way that CSA members can directly create breakdowns and post audition notices. This is a goal for IMDb. At time of press, there are some casting notices on IMDb, but the 'Pro Casting service' is not in wide use among CSA members. Actors should stay vigilant about how this service develops in the future.

IMDbPro is useful for research. You can learn about films that are shooting in your area by doing a search on your IMDbPro account. Research what films are in pre-production and section the search by location. Once you figure out a film is shooting in your area, the best step from there is to contact the casting director. If she isn't listed, contact the producer, and emphasize that you are a local hire and ask whom to contact. He will want to connect you with the right casting director because he'll know he can save money on local cast.

The other great advantage that a Pro account provides is the ability to look up contact details for producers, casting directors and other industry professionals that you might not otherwise be able to find. Additionally you can make yourself and your own agents' details transparent for colleagues who may be trying to contact you.

Actors spend a lot of time moaning about IMDb, so what is the problem?

Actors are forever complaining about IMDb and its lack of user friendliness. I have done my own share of kvetching about it. It's so important to our careers yet it is impossible to locate a single human being to speak to and reason with about the listing of credits. Actors are saying 'IMDb! It's ruining my career!' Actors are dramatic of course – it goes with the territory.

The objective of IMDb is to be as comprehensive and as accurate as possible. The objective of actors is to forward their careers. Herein lies the rub. Note that these objectives are not the same. While actors want and need to use IMDb as a tool to market themselves and enhance their job opportunities, IMDb is a behemoth with a mechanical, impartial personality. It doesn't care if you look good or not, as long as your credits are listed accurately.

I'm not sure that IMDb has ruined any acting careers but I can say for sure that there are times when it can have a negative effect. One of the biggest actor complaints is that they cannot *remove* credits. Unfortunately many of us have credits that we are less than proud of. A good friend of mine, early in his career when he was needing money, signed a contract with an ostensible action film called *Cracker Jack 3*. By the time the film was printed and merchandised, the title listed on IMDb was *Girl Camp: Lesbian Fleshpoints*. His brother wrote to him and said, 'I guess I know what I'm getting Mom for Christmas!' and his agent was less than thrilled. Needless to say, he was not so happy about these credits and wished he could remove them. But alas . . . IMDb does not care about his career. It only cares that he appeared in these films with the unfortunate titles. It only cares about facts, not actors' careers.

This actor does not include these films on his own resumé, but since that time, he has collected so many more credits to his name, that these silly titles have fallen to the bottom of the heap, largely unnoticed. So I wouldn't say that *Girl Camp: Lesbian Fleshpoints* has compromised him.

Unfortunately, however, that is not always the case. I was once developing a feature film with a production company. The private source of funding was a Texas family with very conservative values. One actor had auditioned brilliantly and the director wanted to hire him. When the producer checked the actor's credits on IMDb, he called me and said, 'There is no way we can make the offer. As soon as the funders see that he has a credit called *"Young People Fucking"* they will not hire him.' When I reported this to the actor's agent she said, 'That title was just an ironic joke – not a porno film!' Furthermore, the released title had been *Y.P.F.*, not *Young People Fucking*, which was only an early name that was later dropped. Well, do you think we could get them to change this on IMDb? It is impossible to get anyone on the phone to explain the situation. They have not, in fact, answered any of my pleas for an interview for this book, and the CSA coordinator just sighed, 'There is no customer service.' So hence this actor wasn't hired and for a very silly, unfair reason.

The other frequently encountered problem is that IMDb confuses people with the same names, resulting in actors getting credits for things they didn't do. If you are early in your career, look on IMDb and see if there is already someone working in the industry with your name. Try to avoid this problem by adding an initial or middle name, to make your name distinctive, and use it when making all acting contracts.

Lastly, IMDb insists on keeping records of people's ages. For years I've been lecturing actors not to reveal their age, but their playing range. Well, this throws a wrench into that! An actor even sued IMDb over this and lost the case. She claimed that outing her true age hindered her career. (Please see Chapter 26 with details about actors stating their age.) Yes, it's true that an actor's age is a fact, but so is her blood pressure, shoe size and star sign. Yet these other attributes are not listed. Would it be a lie to simply not mention an actor's year of birth? There are also concerns of parents of child actors. Why should their child's age and place of residence be exposed publicly? Can we take IMDb to task for this? I hope some ambitious entertainment lawyer may try again.

What actors should _not_ do when interfacing with IMDb

When updating your information, try not to be anxious and impatient about when it actually gets posted. There is some lag time between when you update it and when it appears. One actor I talked to was complaining that they didn't update him fast enough, and this was preventing him from getting hired, or negotiating higher salary. So he sent IMDb a nasty correspondence which he claims made them even slower at adding his credits.

Don't try to enter incorrect or embellished information. This will only flag you as an unreliable source. The data entry staff rate submitted history, so if you've previously listed yourself as credited, for example, in a non-credited role, they won't trust you the next time, even when you're submitting a factual attribute.

Deleting information on IMDb can be a frustrating and vain exercise. Instead, try to correct it.

Don't obsess about your Star Meter rating. The Star Meter measures an actor's popularity based on how many hits she scores weekly on her IMDb page. The lower the number, the more 'popular' an actor is. Some actors become obsessed with the measurement and take to constantly hitting their IMDb page or asking friends/family (strangers on the bus) to look them up in order to improve their numbers. I have not done an official survey, but in my experience of moderating panel discussions and exchanging with colleagues, casting directors do *not* cast according to IMDb Star Meter numbers. At one point there were accusations in the press that Star Meter ratings were rigged, and a number of third party companies surfaced that promised you that for a fee they would lower your Star Meter rankings. IMDb has officially discredited these companies, so run away if you are approached by anyone who offers money in exchange for an improved Star Meter ranking.

An actor's worth is valuable at box office but it is a mystery to all of us in the industry exactly how to estimate an actor's worth since he is only as good as the numbers on his last film. Personally, I would much rather cast according to an actor's ability rather than his Star Meter rating or his ostensible box office worth. The film business is, however, exactly that – a *business* – so producers and networks care very much about an actor's ability to be 'hot' at the box office. Sales agents think they know which actors are the most valuable, even when the list of 'A' actors versus 'B' actors is always changing and shifting. Casting directors are constantly fighting with producers and sales agents about who would be right for a role, based on talent rather than numbers but in any case, the IMDb Star Meter is not the key factor.

Things to remember from this chapter

- IMDb is a powerfully important tool for an actor and her marketing strategies.

- Make friends with IMDb by becoming a conscientious contributor to the factual accuracy of the site.

- Invest in an IMDbPro account.

- Actors should be wary about films they choose because dodgy titles can compromise an actor's legitimacy.

- Be proactive about looking for work on IMDb.

PART THREE

The world market

We live and work in an international market. I interact with actors, producers and directors from all over the world. Globalization brings us more opportunities but often we find ourselves overwhelmed with possibilities of where to live and work. In this section, I will explore the opportunities that actors have to work internationally.

PART THREE

The world market

21

Where to live as an actor and other conundrums

Some actors are plagued with the question about where they should live in order to get the most work. There was a time when actors who wanted to work in film automatically moved to Hollywood. In today's world, where the Internet brings us so much closer, this is not such a foregone conclusion.

When I was young, one of my teachers taught me that a happy person is a person who loves:

- what they are doing;
- where they are living;
- and who they are with.

All of these factors must be somehow weighed and balanced when you decide where to live. True enough that location is important, but you also need to measure this against what you do and whom you are with. Presumably if you're an actor, you know what you love to do: act. You have to figure out where you can act the most, which is not so obvious.

If there is acting work in your home vicinity, you may end up working more as an actor and less as a waiter than you would if you lived in Los Angeles. Perhaps in order to live with your partner, you have to live in a certain place. How can you find acting work and live with the person you love? Can the person you love make compromises and allow you to fly away for acting jobs? These are complicated life decisions that can't be answered in this book, but perhaps this chapter can help you weigh your options.

Is Hollywood Mecca?

When I worked with Guillermo Del Toro, I asked him if he lived in Los Angeles. I figured that any director as successful as him would live there and he said, 'I hate Los Angeles! If the whole world fell into the ocean, except for Los Angeles and that was the only place in the world left to live, I still wouldn't live there!'

In my classes, actors often ask me, 'Should I move to Los Angeles?' Many of my students are Europeans, but I would answer North Americans the same way. The first question I always shoot back is, 'Do you like Los Angeles?' Would you really consider moving to a city that you have never been to before? Try visiting the city first.

Los Angeles is not the only place for an actor to live and while Hollywood is universally known as the entertainment capital of the world, ironically not so many films and TV series actually shoot there anymore. Production budgets may dictate that the film shoot elsewhere. Thanks to tax incentives, local industries in many US and Canadian regions are booming with production, giving small town actors breaks into the business. Europe also hosts popular locations, especially if the story takes place there.

Working locally

Local actors are offered day player roles, but can often take a shot at bigger guest star and recurring roles as well. It is to the production's advantage to cast locally, dodging transportation and accommodation costs to bring in Los Angeles actors. With the advent of tax incentives in various states, SAG re-configured the rules to encourage the hiring of local actors in the USA. This means that even while local actors aren't always paid for travel days, they can petition to get reimbursed for mileage within a 500-mile radius of their hometown. In some cases they can get accommodation expenses and per diem too. For example, there are actors auditioning in New Orleans and driving to Atlanta for shoots, while Pennsylvania actors commute to Michigan, and Seattle actors are considered for shoots in Portland, Oregon.

If you are North American and live in a production area, working in your local market first is an excellent way to build your resumé before moving to Los Angeles. It can work the other way around too. There are actors who move to LA but still stay in touch with their regional casting directors for auditions. If an interesting role comes up, they self-tape and fly back to shoot.

My former student, Sarah Marie Brown, pre-booked several jobs back in her hometown in Ohio while in Europe attending the Prague Film School. She stayed in touch, auditioning online and by Skype. Now she has moved to Los Angeles but often finds herself flying back to Cleveland to work.

Clearly identify on your promotional materials and online profiles the cities where you can work as a local hire. If you have an aunt who you can stay with in Detroit, and don't mind springing for the plane fare . . . there's a lot of stuff shooting in Michigan. On your Actors Access profile, you can write based in 'Los Angeles/Detroit.' Spotlight in the UK also allows actors to write 'London/Edinburgh', for example. I know one LA-based actor who even simply writes that he is willing to work as a local hire anywhere that they may be shooting. He claims that this opens a lot of doors for him, but he does need to cover his travel expenses.

In the European Union, which is a free work zone for talent holding EU passports, actors are sometimes willing to fly themselves to various countries for shoots, even if it means that they only break even on costs. It is a good idea to inquire about tax withholding since it can vary from country to country. Working in another city is a way to add scenes to your show reel, and make connections for further work.

Is NYC Mecca?

'Los Angeles or New York City?' many actors ask. The common wisdom is that actors make their film breaks in Hollywood but hit it in theatre on Broadway. New York City booms with independent film, and many casting directors are bi-coastal. So if you're looking to move to the USA and you're trying to weigh up where you should live, a good first question to consider is – *do you drive?* If you live in Los Angeles, this is essential. In New York – not so much. Gotham City and Tinsel Town are as different as two cities can be except in one way . . . both are extremely competitive. If you want to live in New York or Los Angeles, make sure that you enjoy competition. Yes, there are many jobs and opportunities in both places, but there are also many more actors fighting for them. Be prepared to walk into the waiting room at an audition and see hundreds of actors who look just like you. If you move to either city, make sure you have money in your savings account to start, and be prepared to take on a non-acting job. The bigger and more competitive cites also tend to be more expensive as well. The real question depends on quality of life. There are very few actors who make their living only from acting. Most supplement their living with PR jobs, teaching, coaching, clowning work, etc.

In truth, film and TV casting is done from everywhere. Back in the 1990s when I was working with kids in Chicago, I was directing a young boy named Jeremy Sisto in a theatre performance, but before I knew it, I had lost him to play Kevin Kline's son in his first break, *Grand Canyon*. It is nothing new for actors to be cast outside of LA on studio productions, and regional casting directors are often called upon to help LA casters do broader searches. For example, I was asked to do a sweep of Europe when Andy Whitfield was sadly unable to play Spartacus any more. Meagan Lewis, CSA from New Orleans, regularly works with director Steve McQueen, even when he's not shooting in the South East, simply because he likes her taste in actors.

From abroad . . .

British and Australian actors used to fly to Los Angeles for Pilot Season and now Pilot Season comes to them. American casting directors are always posting their breakdowns in London and Sidney as well. American TV series are rife with international talent. The Internet is what makes all of this possible of course. Via Actors

Access, Eco-Cast, and Castit, actors are submitting themselves from every state. (See Chapter 18 on Internet casting.) One of my favourite examples of a British actor, cast from London, was when Suzanne Smith found Hugh Laurie for *House*. He was shooting something in Asia at the time, and he pointed a wobbly camera at himself in the hotel room. This was before it was so easy to upload tape to a computer so he had to post it via snail mail as a bulky VHS tape to his agent, who then had to convert it from PAL (European format) to NTSC (American format) and send it along to the network. He wasn't cast directly from the tape, but it's what got him the invitation for a callback.

Canada

Vancouver and Toronto are both booming film markets, not only for Canadian film, but also for multiple US series and features that shoot there as well. Canada is an easier place than the USA for British actors to get work papers. When American films shoot in Canada, they often are working on a tax incentive programme called CAVCO, which requires that a certain amount of the cast be hired from Canada. So in that case Canadian actors win. Canadian actors wishing to work in the USA must be cast directly from the US production, in which case production handles work papers. Otherwise, Canadian actors can apply for O–1 visas as discussed in this section. Conversely Americans wanting to work in Canada must have a Labor Market Opinion (LMO). This is a document that ostensibly proves that no Canadian actor could have played the role that you were cast for, and the document must accompany you when you come through customs.

If you are not American, and want to work in America

The United States is not the only place in the world for actors to work, and it's not even the largest film industry, with both Europe and

India surpassing it in the number of films produced per year. Many international actors we know, like Aksel Hennie from Norway, Mads Mikkelsen from Denmark and Juliette Binoche from France, made their name at home first, fast tracking themselves into the American market. International actors geared towards the hyper-competitive American scene must have stamina, passion and break-back perseverance. They also need to confront the bureaucratic process of applying to work in the US.

If you want to work in the USA, you need to find a way to officially become 'an alien of extraordinary ability'. In other words, you need minimally an O–1 visa, which is the legal documentation that a non-resident artist must obtain to work in the United States. The O–1 is specifically designed for 'foreign nationals of extraordinary ability in the arts . . . or motion picture or television industry'. Essentially, the artist must petition for this visa, proving that she is an expert in her field. Expertise is determined by awards, and documentation of critical and/or commercial success. Letters of recommendation from industry professionals such as casting directors, producers, or directors corroborate an actor's standing and strengthen the application. A successful application will require time, money and a good American emigration lawyer. There are many firms that specialize in smoothing the process. A manager on the US side, who can support your application, is another essential asset.

If you are hired from Europe, then the production will organize the papers for you, but they may or may not extend to other productions. The O–1 visa is sufficient for many productions but some studios (NBC/Universal and Sony, for example) demand a green card, which is much more complicated to obtain. Do not even think about going to auditions without the paperwork. You will not make friends if you start shooting a project when you are not legal to work.

Meg Liberman (Senior Vice President of Casting at CBS Television Studios) recommends: 'If a foreign actor is hired by a production company using their Visa to work on a particular production, that Visa might not extend to another production company. The best thing to do is acquire a "Blanket O–1" (not specific to any one project), the language on the underlying paperwork should state that the Visa will work for "any and all film and television projects".' One casting department learned the hard way after hiring a foreign actor on a series for NBC (the production company was CBS studios) using his Visa, then hiring the same actor on another series not produced by CBS Studios called 'Las Vegas', also for NBC. The second production company didn't accept O–1 visas at all. Unfortunately, they had shot a few scenes with this actor before they realized that they didn't have the appropriate paperwork, subsequently he was fired and replaced. It cost the production hundreds of thousands of dollars to re-shoot; needless to say, no one was happy.

If you are American and want to work in Europe

For North American actors wanting to work in Europe, it's the same situation flipped over. Americans need emigration lawyers also to help them apply for their work visas in the European Union. Laws vary from country to country, and if you are a resident and legal to work in one EU country that does not necessarily extend to the next.

There is one American actor who I know who has relatives in Europe and is brilliant at getting hired as a 'local' cast member on productions that are shooting there. He keeps in touch with European casting directors, self-tapes and offers to fly himself to locations. He claims to break even on expenses as he flies on air miles and the work is always worth it. He dodges SAG rules by working 'Financial Core', so he is able to work legally on a SAG project as a non-SAG contract.

Things to remember from this chapter

- When deciding where to live, weigh all factors in your life. If you wish to move to Los Angeles, New York or London, then you're an actor who must love and thrive on competition because while there is more work, there are also more actors. Many actors have built successful careers in alternative locations using creative marketing and submitting on-line auditions. If you wish to live in a foreign city, make sure you apply for the appropriate work papers.

22

Success stories: Actors who live and work internationally

In this section I've created a patchwork of stories by actors who work across borders. Just to reiterate the fact that there is no recipe for success and our career paths in the entertainment industry are often meandering, I asked some actors I know to share their experiences, and choices of where to live. (They all happen to be male, so I apologize to my female readers that I haven't provided any female examples, but they certainly do exist.)

Experiences of a European actor who made the move to Los Angeles

Miraj Grbic was born in Bosnia, and he lived in Sarajevo through the longest siege of the twentieth century, dreaming the entire time of a career as an actor. He has been very successful in his own region, where he has played in films and starred in TV series. When he walks down the streets in Balkan countries, he is always recognized by fans, and stopped for constant photo ops. One of his early breaks came when he played a mean-guy Serbian role alongside Richard Gere and Terrence Howard. This opportunity came thanks to *The Hunting Party* shooting in Croatia. I taped him for *Mission*

Impossible while I was in Sarajevo for the film festival. The role he actually auditioned for went to someone else, but I saved the tape and at the last minute as we were about to start shooting, the writers decided to add a new comic character to the prison break scene. I showed the tape to Tom Cruise and he recognized Miraj's comic potential immediately. A few years after *Mission Impossible*, Miraj decided that he wanted to rise to the challenge of working in Hollywood, so he and his wife, Maria Omaljev, who is also an actor, took the plunge.

Here is his story, in first person, written seven months into his Hollywood experience.

I will try to share my LA experience with you, and give you some hints on how to survive in this city. When I arrived here, I heard things like 'LA will chew you up and spit you out'. Well . . . It is like that, but not always.

When I landed in LAX, my only thought was 'I want to go back home!' But after seven months in the City of Angels I did one feature, two short movies and I am working on two TV Shows for 20th Century Fox and Paramount Pictures. My wife, Marija Omaljev, just got a recurring role for a new sitcom pilot, where she auditioned for a co-star role and they cast her for a recurring role.

So I will tell you something about moving from Europe to LA. Do not move here when you are thinking about it. Move when you know that it is the right place for you to be. If somebody told you that no one will give a damn about projects you did in Europe . . . well, it is true. But sometimes, it is not. I can't really talk about that, because I was lucky enough to get cast from Europe on *Mission Impossible IV: Ghost Protocol* and as soon as I came here, people knew who I was.

If you are an academy-educated actor, with a lot of experience, that will help you in the pre-read, because there are no cameras there. If you are a great actor, people here will see that. This is HOLLYWOOD, and YES, this is a centre of our business. These guys know their job.

Don't come to LA without money, or be ready to find a second job, because life here COSTS. We were lucky and worked continuously on big shows for years before we moved here. If we hadn't had that money, I would have had to work to be able to audition.

Try to find proper representation before you come here. If you don't have that, it will be very hard to get an audition. Submit to Actors Access and LA Casting. It is a good way to find auditions, but also a good way for some agencies to find you. If you find an agent and if they tell you that you have to pay more than 10% – or that you need new headshots that you have to do with their photographer, costing about 500 dollars, run like your hair is on fire. It is the twenty-first century, so Google them. It is the city where about 100,000 people arrive every month and 100,000 people leave. There are many scams, people will try to take your money on headshots or on acting schools. Don't let people teach you acting when you can teach them.

I also know you are wondering about one particular thing and that is the accent. You don't have an American accent and no matter how good your accent is, they will know that it is not authentic. Don't consider that as a flaw but as an advantage. Out of 300 people at the audition, five of you don't have American accents. Consider yourself unique, but at the same time, work as hard as possible to lose it. My wife went to an audition for a new sitcom pilot for an American part and she has a slight accent (for me unrecognizable) but the producers, after they saw her audition, changed the script to make the role European.

Be prepared for every audition. Be ready in every moment. This is the city where life is changing every second. Most of all, believe in yourself. That is an LA religion. If you don't want to be here, stay where you are. If you know that you belong here. Come!

I wish you all luck! Aim for the stars and reach the stars.

The proliferation of film incentive programs means more projects are shooting outside of LA and NYC and advances in technology have made it possible to audition remotely so there are more opportunities nowadays for regional actors.

LANA VEENKER, Portland, Oregon

Karel Roden decided to stay in Europe

Karel Roden is an example of an actor with an international career who has chosen to live at home in the Czech Republic.

He was already a star in his country in 1998 when he landed a role opposite Robert de Niro in *15 Minutes*. Immediately several Los Angeles agents tried to snap him up. He was advised not to take the first one who came along. He eventually settled with Endeavor Management, which subsequently merged with William Morris. He also collaborates with Lou Coulson and Associates in London, to help him pick up work on his side of the pond.

Karel subsequently picked up roles on *The Bourne Supremacy* with Matt Damon, *Running Scared* with Paul Walker and *Mr. Bean's Holiday*, just to name a few. His agent urged him to move to Los Angeles and he definitely would have qualified for an O–1 visa, if not a green card, but he held out.

'I don't want my whole life to be about following a career,' he says. 'There are other things in life.'

Karel decided to stay home, where he can enjoy his friends, his family and his horses. He enjoys playing theatre as well as film in his own language.

He enjoys playing in English films because the actors whom he works with challenge him, but the downside for Karel is that the roles he's offered are often the same: Russian Mafia. He feels that maybe if he had made the move to LA and gone to more meetings, made more connections . . . maybe he would have had a greater variety of roles to play. But still he has no regrets. 'Life is short. I don't want to look back and say I did a few movies. I want to enjoy life.' At time of press, he was just celebrating the birth of his second child.

Does it matter that he's in the Czech Republic and not Los Angeles? 'No,' he says. 'When people call to check my availability, they never know where I am anyway. I can't go to a lot of meetings from here but I can self-tape.' So he does, often.

James Babson's story

James Babson also shows us a meandering career trajectory that in some ways is the mirror opposite choice to Miraj and Karel. He chose to work abroad first, rather than at home – not the path well trodden, and his choices led him in unexpected directions. He is now a jobbing actor in Los Angeles, but he never expected to be there.

I was two years out of drama school living in New York City, scratching by on meagre theatre work, when I got a phone call from some friends who were living in Prague at the time. They were doing a production of *Hamlet* in English at a newly constructed replica of the Globe Theatre and asked if I'd like to be a part of it. I was looking for a change and wanted to get out of the city for the summer and so off I went. Little did I know this madcap choice would turn into essentially five years of living in Prague. I had no intention of building an acting career in Prague, but I quickly realized that there was a thriving film/theatre community there.

Once I got acclimatized to the Czech Republic and once I investigated my options as an actor, I found that there was an eagerness from producers and directors to find local talent. If you were a local hire, you could save the US or European production team thousands and thousands of dollars. From my point of view, having done very little film and television at that time, I was more than eager to exploit this. Accessibility was another major component in helping me get work as an actor. Once I was able to be introduced to the local casting directors and agents, I found myself being considered for nearly all major films shooting in the country at that time. Because of my acting experience and training and my excellent command of the English language, I was well positioned. I was very aware, also, that I was cheap non-union labour. Mind you, our low wages were very high in Czech terms so it was a win/win. While in NYC, I lived in a rat-hole with five other guys, while in Prague I had my own large, one-bedroom apartment in a prime neighbourhood. Moreover, I was able to support myself 100% of the time on my craft, rather than in NYC where I had to live off of tips as a bathroom attendant at a club (but that's another story).

In New York I'd have been lucky to even get in the room on high-level projects such as *Hellboy* (where I played a supporting role beside Ron Perlman), *League of Extraordinary Gentlemen* (in which I played a scene with Sir Sean Connery). If I had gotten in the room, it would have been filled with 250 actors. In Prague, there was like eight guys my type I'd go out against. I was very very fortunate to get the jobs I did.

I personally had no previous intention to be a film or television actor. It just didn't even cross my mind. This may sound funny because most of us spend our times watching actors in film and television. Because all the acting I had ever done was onstage as a kid and during my education at Carnegie Mellon University where I received a BFA in acting, I had literally no experience in film and therefore never really considered it. I assumed that I would be a theatre actor and New York City was really the only choice, in my mind. I did work in New York, joined Actors Equity, but the money was slim. So my decision to move to Prague for the summer in many ways provided me the shift that I needed to change my perspective on my career at the time. Totally unexpectedly, I wound up doing more work in Europe in four years than I ever had anywhere else as a professional. So I believe it was far, far more beneficial forging my early path in Europe versus New York.

Once I moved to Los Angeles after nearly six years in the Czech Republic, I had over 10 feature films on my resumé and nearly 20 television commercials, as well as numerous voice-over jobs and several theatre credits. I felt that I was more than prepared to tackle Hollywood. I was right in many ways. I had a good resumé to show off and I could prove to casting directors that I had credits, experience and that I had been working; that I was a viable option as a hire.

However . . .

Los Angeles proved to be more difficult than I ever imagined. I quickly realized that I had been in a very unique position in Prague, being that I was a trained actor in a very small market. More importantly, even though I had many bona fide credits in Hollywood movies, I had not developed relationships with casting directors in Los Angeles. Although I had been working, I was completely unknown among my new colleagues in LA. Actually, I was starting all over again.

There is a lot to be said for being a 'big fish in a small pond', so to speak. But the truth is, except for two or three supporting roles, I primarily played small featured roles during my years in Prague. Although the films were international hits, my work was not powerful, dynamic work. I knew that, as an American film actor, if I wanted to have a career as an actor in supporting and lead roles that WERE powerful and interesting, I would have to work in Los Angeles. It's sort of like Mecca. You have to go at least once. And despite the basic hardships of trying to work as an actor in Hollywood, I do believe it was the right choice to move here. I do make some compromises, however. Even though I work regularly as an actor, I still have to take a 'day' job (in this case, night job at a club) to make ends meet.

J.D. Evermore's story

J.D. Evermore is a perfect example of an actor who has built a professional career outside of Los Angeles. He boasts such prestigious credits as *The Dallas Buyers Club, Django Unchained, 12 Years a Slave*, and *Walk the Line*. He would never have had the unique opportunities to do so without the strength of his foothold in the Southeast, which has been a hotbed of US production. 'Everyone tells me, Dude, you've got a resumé that most every actor in LA would be envious of. But I would never have gotten this far, if I had stayed in Los Angeles.'

In 1990, after reading a book about acting, J.D. set out to Los Angeles to seek out a career as an actor. Well, it didn't go so well. 'I was an idiot,' he confesses, 'thinking that just because I knew someone there in the business that things would go well for me.' It took about two months for him to realize how ill prepared he was, so he moved back to Mississippi to pursue a degree in theatre. In 1995, after working on the set of *A Time to Kill* for a day, in which (now Academy Award-winning actor) Octavia Spencer wrangled him as an extra, J.D. set off to Los Angeles to start a professional career as an actor.

After about a year of rejections and unsuccessful attempts in Hollywood, he decided to relocate to Austin, TX, where the industry was hopping and he was able to finally start building his resumé. He landed his first job by pure luck because he looked like the real-life 'Rape Suspect #2' in *Unsolved Mysteries.* He then managed to book a few movies of the week, and four episodes of *Walker Texas Ranger.*

He tried Los Angeles a few more times but made little progress. In two and a half years, he went through three agents who only got him two auditions. He did manage to land a small role on the fifth episode of *CSI* before the show had premiered, and three episodes of *Days of Our Lives* in an under-five role (under five lines). While this is more success than many Hollywood hopefuls earn, he was nowhere near making a living wage. It was his earnings on a game show that enabled him to keep his head above water.

In mid-2002, J.D. left Los Angeles again and returned home to Mississippi to plan a new path. Shortly thereafter, Louisiana's tax incentives were created and his career slowly began to take off, and by 2005, 15 years after he had read a book about acting, he was finally able to support himself on acting alone. He stayed in the Southeast, commuting and eventually moving to New Orleans where 'You've got a much smaller talent pool and you can pick the low hanging fruit, compared to LA where you're trying to climb the highest tree to get that one small piece of fruit at the top and everyone else is trying to climb that same tree. In New Orleans, I was able to audition for most every major motion picture that came to the state, as well as meet most every major director face to face. That never would have happened in Los Angeles, even if I had been with one of the top agencies.'

J.D. is now in demand in the Southeast. He eventually won a recurring lead role on *Rectify* (Sundance Channel), which shoots in the Atlanta area. For this role, J.D. was likely already competing with other actors from all over the country since New Orleans is more than a six-hour drive to Atlanta. Although production would have jumped at the opportunity to hire him as a 'local', J.D.'s agent resisted and insisted on paid hotel, mileage and per diem. For the second season, his character grew, so production offered him a 'relocation fee' to move to Atlanta. This is something that is very important for an actor to negotiate.

In his early years of acting, J.D. resisted joining SAG as soon as he was qualified, so that he could do union and non-union work and continue building his resumé. (Some actors also avoid joining prematurely because they would rather not pay dues.) J.D. played in thirteen SAG jobs after he was Taft-Hartleyed (invited to join the union) before finally opting to join. He was able to do this because he was living in a *right to work state*. This means that he can legally work a union job without officially joining the union. This is something that actors should research in their own home states. Are you allowed to do a SAG job without joining SAG?

Although J.D. enjoys a successful career, he is not entirely content with his working conditions. 'I can't count the times when I've worked on a show, knowing I've been a working actor all these years and then you get some kid coming from LA whose got three credits to his name, but because he's with a big agent, he's getting paid three, four, five, six times what I'm being paid.'

When I talked to J.D. at time of publishing, he was considering giving Los Angeles one more go, just to 'establish a footprint, and cash in all of the successful shows'. Now that his resumé is so well padded, he feels that he can get a leg-up on stronger representation. Otherwise, he said, 'I'll be making scale plus ten, or barely above that for the rest of my life' (union scale salary plus 10% agency fee).

> In the South-East we say, if you're doing well, let's get you a manager in LA to tag team and then do a year making tapes and if that goes well, have a crack at Pilot Season. But don't move full-time.
> ALEXANDER WHITE, Alexander White Agency, Atlanta, Georgia

English-speaking actors from around the world

The International Alliance of Casting Directories (IACD), a global organization, has made it possible for casting directors to coordinate talent in North America, the UK, Australia, New Zealand and South

Africa. Thanks to online networks such as Breakdown Services and Spotlight, casting directors anywhere in the world can post their breakdowns and get submissions internationally. When you are cast in an American project through this system, normally production will take care of your working papers.

> I think there's a huge value in building up your resumé with regional work before attempting one of the major markets. There may be fewer opportunities, but there is also less competition. It's also smart to find out how you really feel about the work before uprooting your entire life. Not to mention the fact that it's hard enough to get seen by casting in a larger market, but it's pretty much impossible if you have nothing on your resumé.
>
> ERYN GOODMAN, Portland, Oregon

Actors from smaller countries

If you do decide to leave your country and work in America or Britain, you need to learn to break out of your accent and chameleonize yourself to the new culture. Don't lose your specific ethnic identity, however. It can be very valuable as a branding device. Actors like to complain about being typecast but remember that *typecasting* means *casting*. For example, my German friends often complain that if they go to Los Angeles, they often find themselves playing only Nazis all the time. However, they need to measure this up against the problem they might have in Germany, which is that they are just one more actor. That German-ness makes them special in LA. If you're good, you always have the opportunity to break out of that, as Christopher Waltz did. Because he was such a brilliant Nazi on *Inglorious Basterds*, now he can play anything.

At a casting symposium at the Berlinale Talent Campus, an actor from Lebanon stood up and asked, 'Since I come from a region in crisis, and since cinema is practically nonexistent in our country . . . What are the chances and opportunities for an actor from the Middle East to be cast for a film on an international or European level?' On the same day, a Croatian actor asked a similar question.

Any time a region experiences war or crises, it becomes the subject of epic storytelling, in films and TV series. Actors from places like the former Yugoslavia and the Middle East can take advantage of their position. Productions are frequently looking for actors from these regions and because film demands authenticity, casters love finding the real thing – actors who have really experienced the subject matter. The problem for casting directors is *finding* this talent, because often the infrastructure isn't organized enough for agents to emerge. In these regions actors do best to band together and form collective agencies, posting their information on the Internet. I often attend international film festivals as well, specifically looking for actors from other countries. We are on the lookout constantly for new talent.

What about foreign names?

Many actors who want to work in the English-language market wonder if they should change or Anglicize their names. There is no clear and correct answer, except that I would advise actors to consider this issue EARLY in their career, before their credits are listed. I know one actor who decided to change her name after she had already successfully played lead roles in several films. When casters tried to look up her credits on IMDb, nothing came up as if she had never existed. It's true that Americans are not good at languages and when immigrants arrived at Ellis Island, names were shortened inadvertently, but we all learned to say Schwarzenegger. Sometimes just a slight spelling adjustment can help a bit. Note, however, that Gyllenhaal and Chiwetel Ejiofor are also not very easy names to spell, yet we manage to do it. If you have an unusual name, it's less likely that there will be another actor with the same name (thus cutting down on the possibility of confusion between you and another professional).

I wonder what Martin Sheen's career would have been like if he had kept his birth name of Ramón Antonio Gerardo Estevez. Would it have limited him to Latino roles? We will never know. In today's world when multi-culturalism is so prevalent, actors are more confident to maintain their identity.

What about the accent?

While your accent may be precisely why you are being cast, it can be very hard for English-speaking audiences to understand a foreign accent. I have known foreign actors who learned the American accent so well that they've actually had to re-learn their native accent. Even for those who speak English as a first language, regional dialects can be a problem on the broader market. Be as versatile as you can in your dialects to increase your marketability.

23

Regional casting directors

On most large-scale films, there is more than one casting director. We get to know the names of the casting directors from LA who helm the film, because they are listed in the opening credits of the movie. (This was a hard fight incidentally for casting directors even to get recognized and it took many years of lobbying. For more information, see the film *Casting By*, directed by Tom Donahue, which dramatizes this struggle.) Sometimes the main casting director collects the top five A-list talent and then the remainder of the film is cast by a casting director on location. On my first big casting job, a mini-series for the Sci-Fi Network, I cast 83 of the 100 roles. I was disappointed when the credits rolled and someone else's name was in front and if you blinked you missed my name. There are regional casting directors slugging away everywhere and getting very little credit.

> Many of our actors who have moved to bigger markets still audition for us. They keep a good relationship with Detroit.
> KATHY MOONEY, Pound Mooney Casting, Detroit, Michigan

I am not mentioning this so that we can all feel sorry for regional casting directors, but rather to point out that actors do well to learn about and make contact with these 'smaller-name' casting directors because they are often casting more roles. Regional casters can also be more accessible and open than the big name casters. Find the regional casting directors in your area and even within a 500-mile radius. Kathy Mooney, who casts from Detroit, covers actors as far away as Pennsylvania. Research casting directors who work from cities where you can easily work locally, for example, a place where you have relatives or friends. It might mean covering your own travel expenses but it could be worth it for a good role and new connections.

You know a casting director is legitimate when you see CSA next to her name. This means that they are approved by the Casting Society of America and are not allowed to work as an agent (take a percentage from you salary) as well.

European casting directors

I've worked on European co-productions where there were as many as five casting directors from different countries since we had to get named talent from various nations to make the funding work. (For example, German money demands German network stars, etc.)

There are European casting directors who function both as main casting directors in their own countries, but then act as 'regional casting directors' on bigger studio films in cooperation with their American colleagues. If you have a European Union passport or working papers and wish to work in Europe, these casting directors are also good people to research and make contact with for European based work.

Just as the CSA functions to legitimize casting directors in the US, the International Network of Casting Directors provides credentials for casters in Europe. If you are in doubt about a casting director, look her up on the INCD website. http://www.shooting-stars.eu/en/casting_directors_network.php. In the United Kingdom, many casting directors join the Casting Directors Guild of Great Britain.

I know that the bigger roles and the series regulars usually come out of LA, BUT if the actor just wants to be a working actor, I tell them to stay in the South-East and get registered with agents in the various areas. There are many actors who make a living as an actor here in Florida. They combine all of the ways they can act. So one day they may be shooting a feature film, the next a TV series and the next a TV commercial. AND we have a theatre community in Florida. In the Orlando area, a lot of actors work in the various Disney and Universal Parks. Their 'day job' might be working as a character at Disney World, but if they book a TV/film job, they work for a day or week and then go back to their 'day job'.

LORI WYMAN, casting director, Miami, FL

Things to remember from this chapter

- We live in a world market, glued together by the Internet. It is no longer necessary for actors to live in NYC or LA.

- Investigate your opportunities to work in alternative regions.

PART FOUR

Perspectives from the other side of the looking glass

24

The casting director is on your side

The casting director is on your side. This may seem like a contradiction after previous chapters in which I harped on about how casting directors don't like to be contacted too much. It doesn't sound very friendly. But consider this equation:

Actors are afraid of casting directors.
Casting directors are afraid of actors.

An actor once frankly said that he was 'disappointed that I was so dismissive'. I am sure that we do seem that way sometimes, but consider that we can often feel overwhelmed by actors. Furthermore, actors who don't find success often compensate by demonizing the person who they see as the gatekeeper, standing between them and the job. We, casters, can find actors intimidating because they could turn their hostility towards us. (They do, sometimes.) Actors are angry when they perceive themselves to be in a powerless position, and they bring their aggression with them.

While we can feel overwhelmed by actors, at the same time we need actors, good actors, to do our job. Once you've stepped into our office to audition for a role, we are 100% on your side. We truly want you to be exactly right for the role and we do everything possible to make you sparkle and shine. It doesn't always seem that way to actors, however. To them, we may seem rude, evasive or unhelpful. Try being us for a day. Here is a view from the other side of the looking glass. Consider these scenarios.

The casting director's position in the production

I was working with another casting director to cast a supporting role on a major studio production. It was a difficult role requiring a very young actor, who could perform physical comedy. My colleague knew the exact actor and introduced him to the director immediately within the first pool we presented. No matter how persuasively she tried to convince him, the director said, 'No way, keep looking.' Five hundred actors later, she slipped this very same actor into the mix again, and the director said, 'Yes! That's him! You see what happens if you keep looking.' This story epitomizes the frustration of being a casting director. We want dearly to book the role because then our search is over, but it can be a long road until we actually get approval.

Casting directors have to play the game. Everyone who works in production – the special effects team, or the costume department – has her own version of this story. Film is the director's medium. In the beginning of the film era, studios micro-managed productions, overseeing each detail, including casting, at a time when casting directors didn't even exist. In the 1960s European auteur directors started to influence American film. Studio systems gave way to directors like Francis Ford Coppola, and later Steven Spielberg, and George Lucas, who dictated the role of director as king.

In these times we still experience the deification of the director. From a casting standpoint, directors can seem unreasonably petulant and at times sociopathic, demanding more and more choices before they make a decision – like kids in a candy shop wanting to taste each lollypop before they finally choose which one. They seem to take special joy in torturing casting directors and demanding that we bring in hundreds of actors from far reaches of the earth, even when they have an excellent selection of talent in front of their face. Brilliant actors can be overlooked because of an obstreperous director who just wants to see more, more, more.

In some productions, the studio or the ubiquitous network wields the fist of power, more so than the director. Studios sometimes hire first-time directors or no-names over whom they can exercise control. In a TV series, the producer and the network have more say in casting than a director, who is usually a hired freelance on an episode by episode basis. There are times when a casting director is really supportive of an actor but we may have to convince not only the director, but the producer, the executive producer, his wife, the studio casting director, the studio executive and the network head honcho.

More than once I have cut deals with agents, under producer and director approval, only to get a call from the studio demanding that I retract the offer. It's embarrassing for me, and heartbreaking for the actor. Sometimes a director simply changes his mind about whom he wants to cast. Don't take it personally because it even happens to big stars. A casting director friend of mine was in the middle of negotiations when he had to call Kyle McLachlan's agent to reverse course. Kyle McLachlan had his day, however. Val Kilmer was promised the role of Paul Atreides in *Dune*, only to have David Lynch re-think his choice and cast McLachlan, who was a relatively unknown Seattle theatre actor at the time. (Kilmer had already rehearsed and was suffering an eye infection from make-up tests.) Other times the director likes one actor and the producer likes another actor, so it becomes a political battle catapulting the casting director back to the drawing board.

Even while we support actors, we are often helpless to influence these decisions. Be assured that when you walk through the door, we want you to be the one who the director will choose. Then we can book the deal and we have succeeded in our job. Remember that we're on your side at the audition. You're the talent, not us. Every actor who enters the casting room is a potential gem for us to discover. When actors nervously step in for auditions, I wonder why. Why are they nervous around me? I want them to be perfect for the role. Internalize this fact and use it as a springboard of confidence.

Don't buy into the illusion that you are a supplicant standing at the gates of success in a casting director's office. It's true that some actors view castings as capital punishment, going drearily along as if to their own executions. Don't internalize the system's hierarchy or allow casting directors and arrogant industry professionals to destroy your spirit. Believe in yourself and persevere. Director Barry Levinson recounts an early NBC pilot series called *Peeping Times*. The studio told him to get rid one of his actors because he wasn't funny enough. It's a good thing that the actor paid no attention to the studio executives' opinion, before going on to host his own show, one of the most popular comedies in American TV history – *Late Night with David Letterman.*

What do casting directors want?

My objective is to present the director with as many brilliant, castable actors as possible. If I bring him many great actors from which to choose, then I'll look good and we'll cast the film. What do casting directors want? We want the same thing that actors want. We want more jobs on more films. The more we're able to impress the director, the more jobs we'll get. If the actor succeeds in the audition, then so do we.

We are under pressure to present great talent to a diverse panel of difficult professionals who compose the production team. We want that panel to like the actors we bring, so we work hard to present the actor in the best light possible. That is why we give directions. Listen, and really take in our notes, because we're trying to help you. When I was working for Fox Studio they sent out a memo to the casting directors on the project:

> The audition is a tool to get the actor a job.
> The taped audition is a mini commercial for the actor.
> If the audition and taping session doesn't properly sell the actor for the role, there is a problem.

The studio is on your team too. The studio wants the actor auditions to be as good as possible.

On nervous directors

Actors focus on their own nervousness at auditions.
Consider that the casters might be even more nervous.

The casting director is stressed because she may have two hundred people to see in two days. The director is nervous because he's got a producer breathing down his neck, and a hundred million dollar production on his shoulders. Some directors feel awkward around actors. I worked with one director who felt much more comfortable meeting with the special effects department (where he had started his career) than he did meeting talent. He went out of his way to avoid actors, interrupting casting sessions so that he could show me trailers of his last film. During his sessions with actors, he didn't have the slightest idea what to say to them or how to direct them, since acting was so far from his area of expertise.

Actors in my casting workshops often tell me nightmarish stories about rude, disrespectful casting directors. I've heard stories about directors ignoring actors, or taking phone calls during the audition. One actor told me that the casting director's phone was ringing during her entire casting. 'What should I have done?' she asked. I advised her that next time she might say, 'That was distracting for me. May I go again?' (It's part of the 'polite fuck you'.) Another actor complained how the director scowled during his entire performance. Remember, he may not be thinking about you at all. He could be thinking about the fight he had with his wife that morning. Don't let someone else's stress set you off.

Realize that there may be one hundred actors who audition for a given role. Only one will get it but that doesn't mean that the other 99 were poor actors. You may have done a perfectly good audition, but because of these political battles that rage in any production, you didn't get the role. If you felt that the director liked you, then it may be true, but you didn't get the role because the producer wanted his nephew to play it. Don't take anything personally, and move on. The director will remember you for next time.

Things to remember from this chapter

- The casting director is on the actor's side.

- The casting director wants the same thing actors do – more work on more films.

- Casting directors do everything possible to make actors sparkle and shine.

- The casting director has her own stress that may make her *appear* unsupportive.

- There are political battles raging on many productions that are beyond the actor's control.

25

Showbiz ain't fair

Showbiz just ain't fair. It is a wildly random, arbitrary and unfair crap shoot.

In British mini series, *Zhivago*, starring Keira Knightly, we needed an actor to play a one armed, one-legged Russian soldier. After an exhaustive search, my associates and I proudly presented a one-armod, ono loggod, Russian-speaking actor to the director, sure that he would be happy. On top of the tough requirement, we even thought the candidate could act pretty well. When the director saw the tape, he confounded all of our expectations, exclaiming,

'No! No! No! He's wrong for it.'

I was thinking, 'Why? Is the wrong leg missing?'

'He looks like he was born that way! We need someone who was amputated!' he shouted.

Sometimes, an actor can do a perfectly good audition, but he simply doesn't have what the production is looking for. Certain roles have physical requirements. Actors can't get plastic surgery (or amputated limbs) each time they're up for a part. This actor did a good audition, but he didn't match the physical requirements of the role. Although it was shocking to me that the director put such fine a point on it, his prerogative is to be picky. It wasn't the actor's fault. There is nothing he could have done better. In the same way, you might feel that you aced at the audition, but still didn't succeed. What did you do wrong? Very possibly – nothing.

When I first started out, someone told me that talent always rises to the top, but after years of experience, I don't believe it's true any more. I meet many, many talented actors to whom I cannot offer roles. Why? Because acting is the only art form in which the artist is the product. A painter can pour her soul into a painting but the piece is still a physically separate entity from her body. You would never, for example, resist buying a painting because the painter is too short.

Conversely, there are many untalented actors who do get work. It's hurtful for trained actors to live in a world, dominated by reality TV. Some directors lean towards hiring amateurs in an effort to bring authenticity to their films. When I was casting *Everything is Illuminated*, although I found plenty of trained actors, director Liev Schreiber wanted to cast real Ukrainian ditch diggers for one scene. I had to go out on the building sites and find actual Ukrainian workers. He loved them for their authentic look, and imperfect teeth. He didn't seem to mind their inexperience and the faint whiff of alcohol that entered the casting room with them. A trained, professional actor just can't compete in these situations.

Sometimes actors do or don't get cast for silly, non-artistically motivated reasons. One time, I worked on a production in which a very short actor got cut out of a scene, simply because the director couldn't fit him into the same shot with the star, the tall Richard E. Grant. It happens the other way around more often. On *Hellboy*, we were encouraged to find supporting cast members who were under 5'9" because we had to make Ron Pearlman, playing Hellboy, look like a giant. Similarly on *Blade II*, we were discouraged from casting tall actors, for fear of dwarfing Wesley Snipes. The taller actors were rejected and it had nothing to do with talent.

Casting director Maureen Duff claims that when she's casting a leading lady, she tries to find out what the director's mother is like and cast someone who is similar to her. But what if the director doesn't like his mother? So I deduced it to this.

Reason you get cast: You look like the director's mother.
Reason you do not get cast: You look like the director's mother.

The casting process is filtered through whatever unique and unpredictable personal biases that particular director might have. We all possess certain personal qualities. These qualities may be physical – a dimpled chin, or thin lips – or they may be an indescribable part of our chemistry. Michael Chekhov referred to this as creative individuality; 'to create by inspiration one must become aware of one's own individuality'. But because the director also has a creative individuality through which he filters the actor's performance, he might have an association (positive or negative) for that actor's qualities. Danish director Ole Christian Madsen says that in casting you're often 'trying to find someone like yourself, and when you find them you want to cast them again and again'.

In other words, it has to do with personal taste.

> There must be as many Hamlets as there are talented and inspired actors to undertake their conceptions of the character. The creative individuality of each will invariably determine his own unique Hamlet.
> MICHAEL CHEKHOV, *To the Actor on the Technique of Acting*

Even acting skill turns out to be a matter of taste. I introduced an actor named David to a director, who thought he was a terrible actor. Yet when I introduced David to a different director, she thought he was brilliant.

Jiri Machacek is a well known actor in the Czech Republic. I introduced him for a role in *Anne Frank: The Whole Story* and director Robert Dornhelm told me that he was a good actor, but too much like a Russian gangster to fit into the film. Shortly after, I was casting *Black Sheep*, wherein we needed Russian gangsters so I thought, 'Perfect, I'll bring in Jiri Machacek.' Director Joel Schumacher simply said, 'Oh, he's too nice to play a gangster.' So it only goes to show that everyone is screening through their own particular tint of glasses.

These things are personal, but don't take them personally. It matters very little what one person in the industry thinks about you, because everyone's opinion is different anyway. If a director insults you (it happens), develop a think skin, and move on. Do what Meryl Streep did, as reported to me by a *Variety* journalist I know. While in a casting, a famous Italian director turned to the casting director and said in Italian, 'Why do you keep showing me these ugly actresses?' Although Streep understood him, she kept her chin up, completed her audition and then made sure she chatted with him in Italian before she left the room.

In times of equal opportunity, there is no other profession that could get away with this kind of discrimination on the basis of physical looks. This has always been part and parcel of the casting process. When we cast a kid, meant to be the younger version of a character, then they have to look like the star. Other times we have to cast someone who is a mother to another character so they have to look like they could be related. This is good casting, when a family fits together in a convincing way. If you were close but didn't quite make it, this may be the reason you didn't get the cigar.

When you audition, believe in yourself, and your own creative individuality. You don't have any control over these production factors, including what the director is thinking. Surrender to it, and know that even if you don't book the job, that if you work hard and perform well, you may get a role on the next project. You are building a relationship each time you come to the casting.

It's not always about being the most attractive and sexy person around. Unless you're auditioning for *Baywatch*, this is unlikely to be the case. 'You're not pretty enough to be James Dean and you're not ugly enough to be a character actor. So forget about being an actor.' This is what legendary director Billy Wilder said to Billy Bob Thornton while he was waiting tables at a Hollywood party, years before Thornton became the successful actor he is today. 'Do you write at all?' Wilder asked. Thornton replied that yes, he did write. 'Then that's what you need to do,' continued Wilder, 'Create your own way. Don't wait around. Be an innovator and originator.'

What can we learn from Wilder's early advice to Thornton? First, anyone can be a film actor regardless of how they look. Michael Shurtleff in his book *Audition*, reports the producer's first reaction to Barbara Streisand at a casting: 'She sings great, but what can we do with a girl who looks like that?' If you want to be an actor, don't let anyone tell you that you're not pretty enough, ugly enough, tall or short enough. Of course Wilder was wrong about Billy Bob Thornton, so it's a good thing that Thornton didn't stop working at an acting career. Thornton took Wilder's advice, however, and didn't sit around and wait for the phone to ring. He played mostly bit parts until his breakthrough film *One False Move* in 1992, which not coincidentally, he wrote too.

Early in my life, I decided not to be a career actor. Ironically it was partly because of early encounters with casting directors. When I was attending the National Theatre Institute, part of the programme included seminars by lead casting directors from New York City. Typically they were casting soap operas and sported nasty attitudes. They were older mink-clad ladies, draping little dogs on their arms. I remember hearing, 'Look, if you're fat, lose the weight. If you've got a big nose, get a nose job.' I ran away. I hope that no one who is reading my book is running out and getting a nose job or a boob job or any kind of job other than an acting job. If your hair is getting grey, please let it. It's getting harder and harder to find anyone to play the older roles because of our youth-obsessed culture.

When I cast *Oliver Twist*, Roman Polanski wanted people who he considered to be Dickensian-looking. That meant he preferred actors with crooked teeth, warts and wrinkles. The white-toothed models were sent away. When I was casting *Anne Frank: The Whole Story*, I needed kids to play victims in the concentration camp. Parents were contacting me and bragging about their beautiful children. Little did they know that beauty was the last thing we wanted on this film. I needed decrepit, unhealthy, malnourished-looking kids to play scabies patients.

Actors must, at times, let go of vanity. I was once offered the role of an Edwardian era landlady on *From Hell*, a Jack the Ripper thriller, starring Johnny Depp. When I got to set that morning, they sent me to make-up where they first covered my skin in pale foundation, then smeared on black grunge. They proceeded to distress my teeth with a waxy brown paste. Not content with my ugliness, they continued to smear grease in my hair and knot it up. The costume department found a wrinkled old black dress, and when I got to set, a skinny cat was thrust into my arms and he promptly peed on me. At that moment I was introduced to Mr. Depp, and it wasn't exactly my dream scenario. Around that time I realized that I wasn't hired for my looks. Sometimes if you understand this before you go to the interview, it can help you a lot. (By the way, don't look for me in *From Hell*. The scene was cut, at the last minute apparently, according to the Hughes brothers. Did I say anything about the movie business being unfair?)

Things to remember from this chapter

- Showbiz ain't fair.

- Physical discrimination is a normal part of casting.

- Much of casting is determined by the actor's and the director's creative individuality.

- Talent doesn't always rise to the top.

- Actors need to let go of vanity.

- You're making a relationship with the casting director even if you don't book the role.

PART FIVE

Frequently asked questions: the nuts and bolts of casting

Learn the rules so that you know how to break them properly.

THE DALAI LAMA

26

Frequently asked questions about auditioning

Here are the rules. The trick is figuring out when to break them. While I answer these frequently asked questions, there are no formulas for the acting trade.

What can I expect at a film or TV audition?

Be prepared to expect almost anything, and roll with it. Usually for film or TV auditioning, you can expect there will be a camera. There might be several people in the room, or just the casting director and the camera. If it's a large 'cattle' call, they may give you a number before you come into the studio. Usually you need to hold the number under your chin while they take a still photo for identification. Often you are asked to stand neutrally in front of camera, and turn for both profiles before you start reading. (Yes, like in jail, and they've heard that joke before.) In a commercial casting they want to see a toothy smile and your hands, but don't offer this in a film audition or you're screaming, 'I'm a commercial actor.'

Some casting directors may surprise you by handing you another role, or even asking you to improvise a scene that you knew nothing about. Each director has a different process. On *To the Wonder*, Terrence Malick requested improvisations with actors, and then built the role based on the actor he cast (Olga Kurylenko). One of my students said that he was completely thrown when auditioners asked him to speak his lines in Polish. Though he had a Polish name, he didn't speak Polish, so they said: 'So make up a gibberish Polish language.'

What do I say in the introduction?

Often you are expected to introduce yourself in front of camera, for the benefit of the director. This means making a simple introduction, stating your name, agency, perhaps height and mention a few of your best projects. Do not mention your age. Your playing range is all that matters.

The introduction seems to be the hardest part of the audition for some actors. They can't wait to transform themselves into a character but they feel uncomfortable just being themselves for a few moments. To a director this might be the most interesting moment. It's vitally important that you reveal your own personality. *You* are the product and *you* are really the most interesting thing from our side of the camera. 'The actors are my teachers,' commented director Stephen Frears about *My Beautiful Launderette*. He took all of his cues from them since he knew very little about India when he started the film.

If the director is at the audition, he may ask you to say a little about yourself or ask what you have been doing recently. As casting director John Hubbard noted in a symposium I moderated, 'That doesn't mean he's actually interested, so don't go on all day.' It's OK to plan what you'll say in this situation. 'I love to hang- glide and I've been taking advantage of the great weather to do that lately.' That communicates a passion and is something unusual for the director to remember. 'I've just thrown a birthday party for my adorable three-year-old daughter,' is also a good one. It introduces you not just as an actor, but also as mother, or dad. One time an actor told me in his introduction that his cat was having her period. I did remember him but think about *how* you want to be remembered.

Leave problems outside the casting studio door. If you say you've not been doing much, this doesn't give a good impression. The director doesn't want to work with someone who doesn't even take an interest in her own life. If the director asks you what projects you've worked on lately, remember that he doesn't want to hear your entire resumé. Briefly summarize the projects that showcase you well. 'I just got to work with X actor in a BBC series. It was really fun;

we got to shoot in Cornwall. Have you ever been there?' Remember to spin it in the most positive way. Some actors don't feel adequate, and they demote themselves. Turn 'Not much, I was in *Lord of the Rings*, but it was a really small role,' into 'I just worked on *Lord of the Rings*. It was a fantastic opportunity to work with Peter Jackson.'

Never mention negative work relationships at an audition. I've actually seen actors talk us out of casting them by mentioning that they didn't get along with the last director they worked with. Remember that it is a job interview, and we want to work with actors who will cooperate and be team players.

What if I haven't worked much or I haven't worked in a long time?

Being unknown can be a great asset because it means that some agent or casting director can claim that they 'discovered you. Great movie stars have been discovered at times when directors were searching for unknowns. When I was casting *Alien vs. Predator*, I asked director Paul Anderson if we were casting any stars and he said, 'We have two stars. Alien and Predator.' When Steven Spielberg was casting *Jaws*, he said

> I wanted somewhat anonymous actors to be in it so you would believe this was happening to people like you and me. Stars bring a lot of memories along with them, and those memories can sometimes, at least in the first ten minutes of the movie, corrupt the story.
>
> (Peter Biskind's book, *Easy Riders, Raging Bulls*)

Some actors don't break through until later in their careers. Naomi Watts landed the lead in *King Kong* when she was 36. Casting director Priscilla John addressed the issue of the non-working actor in a casting symposium, 'There are plenty of actors who succeed in their 30s or 40s, and you think, "I always knew he'd turn the corner even if he wasn't working much in his 20s, but he's coming into an interesting time."' Casting director Maureen Duff cited the example of Eileen Essell, who has a successful acting career that she started at age 80!

When a director is interviewing you about your career, spin it your way. 'I haven't done much of anything, really. I just got out of school', can become 'I'm hitting the scene now. I just finished a really great programme at X University, or I've been studying with a really exciting teacher, named Y.' Instead of, 'I've only done an unpaid student film,' try 'I just finished working on a really exciting project about a teacher in the inner city, and it was a great role for me.' Remember that the director probably knows that you're inexperienced. Bring your enthusiasm and your self with you.

Who will be there?

This varies. Sometimes it's just the casting director, and sometimes the director will be there too. Director Joe Wright, for example, sat in on every audition when I worked with him on *Charles II* for the BBC. In the US, and generally at film auditions this is less common at the first audition. Old hand casting director, Fred Roos (now a producer) explains that in the 1970s directors (including Francis Ford Coppola and George Lucas) frequently sat in on even the first meeting. Though that's uncommon in these days, be prepared for anything.

If it's a callback, you're likely to have the director, and if it's TV, the producer may come as well. If it's US network TV, your third callback is likely to be a 'test option deal' at which point you read for the Studio. Once you get approved past that point, you read for the network. Meg Liberman, who has cast numerous US network series advises actors in these callbacks to 'replicate the (first) audition', unless directed otherwise.

On rare occasions, the star may be at a callback audition too – mostly if he or she is the producer. Miraj Grbic found this to be the case when he appeared in Prague for a callback on *Mission Impossible IV: Ghost Protocol*. When I ushered him into the room at the Four Seasons, he was greeted by Brad Bird and Tom Cruise. Miraj was nervous but he didn't lose his cool. Tom said to him, 'So I hear you've been in 27 films in Bosnia.' Miraj didn't lose a beat: 'Yes, and I hope this will be my 28th.' Everyone laughed and they immediately knew that they could work with him. He was funny, enthusiastic and he spun himself in a positive way.

The important thing is to do the research, not only on your role and the project, but on who will be at the meeting. Ask, or have your agent find out for you. Know whom you're meeting and what their credits are. See some of their work if possible. It gives you an idea of their style, and a topic of conversation. When I was working on *Wanted*, Timur Bekmambetov took notice of the actors who introduced themselves by mentioning that they really liked his last film, *Night Watch*.

Get to know who the casting director is, her name, and what she looks like. This sounds obvious, but it doesn't occur to a lot of actors. I've had this experience, and it's been corroborated by many of my colleagues. We can meet an actor in a casting on a Monday, but in a café on Tuesday, they have no idea who we are. We meet thousands of actors, so why is it that we remember them better than they remember us? Is it because they're so nervous or preoccupied that they don't see who is in the room with them? Sheila Jaffe, who cast *The Sopranos* among many others, told me that she's gone to cast parties where actors she cast didn't recognize her. Remember the hand that feeds you. Keep up with casting directors and their careers.

> When I go to an audition for a film (we go to auditions too, we don't have to do a piece but I do have to wear a tie and speak in a nice voice), I always try to find out something about the people I'm meeting. I will meet them and say something like, 'I liked that film you did.' You're immediately getting in touch with them. We once met with Robert Altman and just as he was leaving, Ros said, 'I loved the little boy you cast in Popeye' and Altman said, 'Oh, my God, that was my grandson.' And he was so touched that she remembered something like that.
>
> JOHN HUBBARD, casting director

What happens at callbacks?

Great! You got a callback! This means that after your initial audition, you are asked to return. The casting director wants to work with you some more. You may be meeting the director and he might have invited other actors to test who plays well with whom.

To prepare for a callback, know the lines. Callbacks tend to make actors even more edgy since they are that much closer to the role. Some actors do a wonderful first audition, but bomb the callback. They make the mistake of over-preparing, making it impossible to receive direction that might change their original choices. Actors also tend to think they need to prove their acting abilities by showing off, or doing too much, or making that fatal mistake of judging the character. Keep it simple. Know the character, make specific choices, and let it flow.

At callbacks, we're looking at the alchemy of the cast and how they fit together. If you've made it to the callback stage, you don't have to prove yourself. We already think you're a good actor. Often we're assessing your chemistry with another actor or simply your personal chemistry and how it meshes with the role. This is not something that you can push. Either it's there or it's not. My yoga teacher advises, 'The more you relax, the further you'll stretch.' It works at a callback audition as well.

Is it important to get conservatory training or a university degree in acting?

If you get accepted into Juilliard or LAMDA, or another top drama school you've got a great start to your career. These top institutions, by name alone, immediately impress, and lead to invaluable work contacts. Top drama schools, however, are not the exclusive formula to success. In show business there is no proscribed trajectory.

If you want to earn a liberal arts education, then by all means do. This degree could include a specialization in theatre or film. A liberal arts degree is an excellent foundation for acting because history, science and literature are all important when making decisions for building a character. In terms of the real world of show business, however, having a BA or BFA on your resumé doesn't count for much. It's about what you can do. I've never regretted my education, but for jobs I've worked in entertainment, no employer has ever given a toss about my diplomas. I learned on the job. Actors learn on the job too. In olden times when theatre companies travelled, performing from village to village, like the players Shakespeare portrays in *Hamlet*, they didn't have MFAs. They learned their craft through the internship system on stage, and if they didn't perform well, they didn't eat. While I heartily encourage actors to get as much quality training as possible, it does not have to be in a university setting. There are many excellent training programmes and teachers who don't necessarily offer a degree. Natalie Portman famously said, 'I'm going to college. I don't care if it ruins my career. I'd rather be smart than a movie star.' (She is both.) If an actor has no knowledge or life experience, then there is very little from which to build.

I'm a trained actor. Must I keep training even after I have completed my degree work?

Yes. Leonardo DiCaprio, Nicole Kidman and Helen Hunt all have acting coaches. If you think you're a better actor than they are, then skip it. Training is ongoing for actors. Take courses and master classes every chance you get in improvisation, stand-up, Meisner technique, Viewpoints, Shakespearean verse, stage combat, film acting, scene study, audition technique, clowning and physical theatre. Even if musical theatre isn't your speciality make sure that you're studying voice, and dance as well. Being physically fit is important. It's part of keeping the instrument tuned. Acting is physical.

Should I lie about my age?

For some reason actors have this bizarre idea that they should always lie younger about their age, as if the only roles available are for people under 30. On the contrary, one time I was casting a commercial for which we needed 30-something women and a 35-year-old actor announced that she was 29. The director crossed her off his list until I told him later that she was lying. The only thing that matters is your playing range. By announcing your age (your correct age or a fantasy age) you limit your options. Therefore, on your resumé list only your playing range (i.e. 20–30, for example). The playing range should be believable and probably within 10–15 years of your true age.

In the Internet age, it's not possible to hide one's age anyway. Once your age is reported to IMDb, it's impossible to remove. There has been a lawsuit regarding this. Actor Junie Hoang sued IMDb for revealing her true age, arguing that it impedes her job chances. SAG-AFTRA supported her claiming, 'An actor's actual age is irrelevant to casting.' 'What matters is the age range that an actor can portray. For the entire history of professional acting, this has been true but that reality has been upended by the development of IMDb as an industry standard used in casting offices across America.' I wholeheartedly agree with the union, but as of the time of this publication, Junie has appealed but not won the case. For now, an actor must accept this. (More on IMDb in Chapter 20.)

Stick to the age range when face to face with a director though, since he is rarely staring into his computer while interviewing you. In some cases, age range has nothing to do with your actual age. A prematurely bald actor, for example, often plays roles older than himself. Let the casting director lie for you if necessary.

One of the famous examples of an actor playing against his true age is Dustin Hoffman, who played the 18-year-old Benjamin Braddock in *The Graduate*. He was 30, playing opposite Anne Bancroft, only five years his senior, who was meant to be his mother's age. Casting history is full of these examples, so keep your options open.

What do I wear?

The important rule is to wear something that flatters, without upstaging. Casting director Anja Dihrberg notes: 'If the costume becomes more important than the acting, then we have a problem.' Neutral, solid colours work well. No stripes, loud colours, nor white (it reflects the light). Be careful about what jewellery you choose.

We want to cast you, not your earrings. Any hats are bad, as are t-shirts with writing.

Sometimes women feel the need to sex themselves up at castings. While I would advise anyone to play their assets, remember that you want them to notice your acting not your bust line. If it's a particularly sexy role, however, then go for it. For *Van Helsing*, we had a role called 'buxom bar maid', when we encouraged candidates for this role to let it shine. 'There's nothing wrong with wearing a tight t-shirt, if the role requires muscle definition', notes talent manager Derek Power. I generally want to see an actor's waist, whether it is big or small.

Some actors are considered too 'contemporary looking' to play in a period film. A tanned actor who looks great jumping off a surf board in one show, may not be convincing in a seventeenth-century piece. For a period drama, it may be advisable for a man to grow a beard, or whiskers (if there is time) before the casting. Women with dyed or streaked hair, flattened down with hair straighteners are less likely to be cast for period roles as well. Don't broadcast a tattoo; it makes a problem for the make-up department.

For a callback it's advisable to wear the same outfit that you wore for the first audition. You will immediately be recognizable to the director. He short-listed you and he remembers you as the guy in the mauve t-shirt from the first call.

Should I dress as the character?

This question is debated. Most casting directors are happy when an actor suggests the costume somehow. Although you're theoretically auditioning for creative people, don't count on them having a well-developed imagination. Make it easy for them. It's hard for them to imagine you as an investment banker if you're wearing a tie-dye t-shirt. Help them out and wear a suit. Some actors come prepared with a few different clothing options. Be time efficient and make sure you can slip them on and off quickly. Generally, casting directors find it absurd when actors go overboard with costumes. You don't have to rent a doublet if you're up for an Elizabethan era piece. Here are two examples of casting director comments, from a symposium:

I knew an English production company and they went to LA to cast for this commercial and all the actors turned up as Batman. About an hour later the producer turned around and said to the casting director, 'Why are they all dressed as Batman? We're casting a batsman.' I think what you have to do is something that suggests the character, subtly. (A batsman is a cricketer, not a super hero.)

JOHN HUBBARD

I was casting *Tom Brown's School Days* and there was one particular actor who didn't have an agent but kept calling and was desperate to read so we finally let him, and he came in with a nineteenth-century costume. Silver cane and hat and everything and he screamed at the top of his lungs – an awful reading. As soon as he left the room, we all just burst out laughing. But he'd forgotten his silver cane so he had to come back . . .

MAUREEN DUFF

There are simple things that actors do to subtly alter their dress, without turning heads on the bus en route to auditions. A good choice for period drama is wearing an accessory or hairdo that suggests that era. A suit coat for women in a 1940s piece, or a waistcoat for men can go a long way. Be dressed and ready when they call your name. No casting director wants to hear, 'But wait! I have to change.'

Actor Colleen Camp provides a wonderful exception to the 'no elaborate costumes' rule. She was competing against top actors, like Madonna and Demi Moore, for the role of Yvette in *Clue*. At the callback, Colleen came bouncing in wearing a French maid costume and she played the costume so well that from that moment on the casting team couldn't imagine anyone else in the role.

Should I wear make-up?

It's a good idea to even out your skin tone with a light covering of foundation. The camera detects all. Think about the specific role, and what makes sense cosmetically. When we were casting vampires on *Blade II*, Andrea Miltner, who played the first vampire of the film, came to her audition with ghost white foundation, and dark red lips. It helped us to see her as a vampire and she was cast. Sometimes I specifically ask actors not to wear make-up if we're looking for an unpolished look. The things you normally try to hide can be the things that get you cast. When I was acting, a director said to me, 'I want to use the dark circles under your eyes for this role.' Sometimes women overdo their eye make-up. Liner and mascara are designed to accentuate, but too much eye make-up upstages. Bette Davis advised that if you want to bring out your eyes, wear *brown* eyeliner, not black. If your make-up is too thick, you're drawing attention to your liner, not your eyes. Bette Davis, famous for her eyes, should know.

What if I don't know anything about the film?

It's difficult to act in a vacuum. The most important thing, however, is that you can answer the w-questions. Who are you? Where are you? Who are you talking to? What do you want? Very often, the answers to these questions are contained in the sides themselves. If you don't feel like you have enough information to answer these questions, call the casting director's office.

You can request a copy of the script and production may surprisingly be able to provide it. These days, more often than not, scripts are watermarked with your name. It can't hurt to ask. In cases when you are provided with the script, read it! There is nothing that turns a director off more than a missed opportunity.

Often the script is impossible to view, even once you get the job. It used to be only very high profile scripts that required secrecy, but I've had to sign an NDA (non-disclosure agreement) on nearly every film I've worked on in the past several years. Producers are more neurotic than ever about their content being leaked. On *Mission Impossible IV*, I was not even allowed to look at the script until I had been working on the film for several months. The director and producers described the characters they needed, and we used dummy scenes. I felt like a secret agent myself as I finally viewed the script, printed on red paper, and without my cell phone (so I couldn't photograph the pages). I had to go into a clandestine room, where the script was pulled from a locked vault.

There is an example of one of the dummy scenes we used given in Part One. You can see from this scene that all the information you need is contained in the scene. Nevertheless, I did get lots of silly questions from actors. I could only reply that I knew as much about it as they did (since the scene wasn't even real). At some point, you have to take a leap of faith, make decisions and believe in yourself.

Research the project as much as you can in advance. That means knowing the director's previous work, reading the project synopsis, learning something about the historic period in which it takes place, or reading the novel on which it's based. This will give you an intelligent and curious approach to the work. The more you know, the better you will perform.

I need to do this research for my work too. When I worked with Korean director Bong Joon-ho on *Snowpiercer*, I was delighted to watch the films that had made him famous (*Host* and *Mother*). I observed his distinctive, epic style of storytelling. Characters appear in pivotal cameo roles to tell the hero's story. I could see his style and how it related to his taste in casting and acting style. I also found common ground with him in my interview.

Where do I look? Do I look at the camera?

Film generally follows the dictums of Realism, the concept of removing the fourth wall of a room. Just as actors in a Realist play do not look at the audience, we rarely see actors looking directly at camera in film. The performer is not supposed to be aware that she is being photographed, so why would she be looking into camera? Unless specifically required, it is better to look next to the lens. Often the reader is positioned there anyway. If the reader is sitting in a place that is disadvantageous, then choose a spot next to the lens. You don't need to maintain eye contact with the reader. Which is your good side? You should know this if you want to be a film actor.

Figure out which side of your face photographs better and play to that side. Bear in mind that you don't have to fixate on one focal point for the entire reading, but be as generous with your eyes as possible.

Screen acting is in the eyes so we must see them. During the actual filming, the director shoots a scene in all sorts of ways. The actor might be crouched down low, in semi-darkness, or the director may shoot over an actor's shoulder to get a Point of View (POV) shot. Let the director make these artistic decisions when she's shooting the film. When you're at an audition, however, the goal is to show yourself. That means uncreative blocking; play to camera and find a focal point right next to the lens.

When referring to, or seeing something off camera, place it near the camera lens also. Often actors choose a focal point that is either on the floor (wrong! – the eyes go down) or way off to the side (wrong! – then we don't see your eyes at all but only your profile) or even behind them (great, if you want us to see the back of your head.)

Figure out who you're talking to and where they are. Make these decisions before you come into the room. Orient yourself, 'OK, so the camera is there and my mother is to the left of camera and my father is to the right of camera, etc.' Actors sometimes get lost with these logistical considerations. The scene doesn't have to make geographical sense; let the director worry about that later. Play towards camera and locate yourself in the scene. No one will hold your hand through this process.

Is it important to be word-perfect or off-book?

In Part One, I emphasize that it is more important to know the *scene* rather than the *lines*. I encourage actors to learn lines, but to hold the script on their lap. There are two reasons for this; first, you have the script there in case you corpse a line, and second, it reminds me that the audition is a process, a reading, rather than a finished product.

There is one well-regarded acting coach in Los Angeles who encourages actors NOT to learn their lines in order to keep them fresh. Many casting directors, however, will say that it is absolutely imperative to be 100% off-book. In some European countries, the casting director would even kick you out of the room if you don't know the lines. So it's important to know your market. There are actors in Los Angeles who go to three auditions per day. In that case, proficient sight reading becomes an actor's best friend. Some actors only go to a few auditions per month and are given the text well in advance. If that is the case, then by all means learn the lines. It is paramount in either case, that you are prepared.

Film and TV actor William Fichtner told me that if there is only one piece of advice he gives actors new to the craft, it's that the top of your head isn't interesting. He has a point. How can we get to know you if we can't look you in the eyes? If you're reading the text, then your head is bent down. Practise sight reading so that you're ready for someone to randomly throw a script at you, but keep your memorization skills in tune as well.

Is it important to be word-perfect on text?

My advice also goes against the 'dead letter perfect' dictum, emphasized at British training schools. While working with Ian Richardson on *From Hell*, he told me that he found the lines awkward, because although this Jack the Ripper story took place in Victorian London, it was written in an American cadence of speech. He felt, however, it was his professional obligation to make the lines work, as written, so that he did. There are times when actors change lines slightly to make them flow better and some writers/directors go along when the changes improve the product. I've been in castings when the writer actually took notes on the actor's mistakes, wondering if it sounded better with alternative wording. Other writers might have a thermonuclear meltdown when even one line is changed.

No matter how much you prepare, however, you cannot anticipate how much the scene will change and evolve. It is the very nature of television drama that the text is more like a blueprint than a cemented structure. While acting in television mini series I've memorized pages of script only to have it re-written on the day. For both NBC's *Revelations* and ABC's *Anne Frank*, the writers were present on set and re-wrote the lines by hand, passing them to me on the back of a call sheet. If this happens to you at a casting, or on set, don't let it throw you. If you memorized the scene, meaning the *happening* in the scene, and the character's objectives, the scene will run smoothly.

What about accents?

When an accent is required, you have to speak convincingly on the day of the audition. Otherwise the director won't believe that you can do it. Dialect CDs are available. Gillian Lane Plesha, for example, is a respected dialect coach who offers a range of voice products for learning various accents. Have at least a few different accents under your belt. If you're British, then standard American is important. Conversely Americans should learn RP (Received Pronunciation or Standard British). Concentrate first on the accents that will be the most useful to you. If you're a white actor, you probably won't ever be expected to speak in a Chinese accent. (Believe it or not I have actually seen this on a resumé.) Only list the accents that you really have mastered. Often actors think they can do accents well, when actually they sound like cartoons. Get your accent approved by either a native speaker or a dialect coach.

If it's Friday and you've got an audition on Tuesday that requires a new accent, then do whatever you need to learn it. Rent a film that uses that dialect, or find a radio programme on the Internet. If your audition is tomorrow and you just can't master the Irish accent in time, then be honest. It's better to use your own accent and confess, 'I don't know the accent now, but I'm very happy to learn it.' Poor accents can ruin the audition, especially if you're concentrating only on the accent and nothing else. The dialect has to be second nature to you.

> In my jobs, I prefer you enter already in the accent. Don't wait for someone to say 'Now go into the Birmingham accent.'
>
> ROS HUBBARD

What about volume? Must I project my voice?

Actors who come in projecting give themselves away immediately – theatre actor. Theatre actors must throw their voices to the stalls. In film it's important to play to the microphone. If you are speaking to someone who is only a few feet away, speak relatively quietly. If the mic is one metre away, then adjust your voice accordingly. Occasionally there is a separate mic, on its own tripod or even attached to your clothing. In these cases, keep your voice at realistic levels. If you think the character would be whispering for some reason, then whisper. If your character is talking to a large crowd, then use the full strength of your voice.

Shall I follow the stage directions in the script?

Identify when the stage directions are important. For example, if the scene is about one character handing over money, that's a stage direction that is easy to follow in the audition room.

Generally, however, you should ignore the stage directions for two reasons. First the writer is often trying to direct the actors, or tell the director how to direct the scene. When they insert adjectives in parenthesis like 'stunned', 'perplexed', 'hurt', etc. – ignore these. They are result-oriented directions that won't help you act the scene. Stick to the objective and stray from adjectives provided by the writer. Sometimes you will see punctuation that dictates a certain performance. A dash in the middle of a word usually means the character has more to say but is cut off. In these cases be prepared to have more to say in case the other actor or reader doesn't cut you off. Sometimes writers will capitalize an entire line, which seems to mean that they want you to scream. You're the actor, so you make the choices about the performance. Above all, make the scene work.

The second reason to ignore stage directions is that the writer might also be trying to tell the casting director how to do his job (these pesky writers are going too far.) Andy Pryor, who casts

Dr. Who and many BBC TV shows, was embarrassed to call in actors for the role called 'Fat Bitch'. The role name was a way of describing the character as unpleasant, but there are many ways to devise this through the acting. What's more, you might get the side and think, 'But I'm not fat!' (or blond, or whatever). I've called thin actors in on 'fat' roles, simply because I thought they could act the role. The writer's description of physical attributes throws actors off. So just ignore it! (My apologies to my writer friends.)

The audition is artificial. The way we shoot a scene at a casting may be entirely different from how it will be shot in production. If the scene takes place in a car, we don't go out to the parking lot and shoot in a car. A walking scene is hard to film without a dolly and grip department, so be prepared to say the lines standing in place. If there are stage directions like 'they kiss', then make the scene work without kissing the casting director or the reader. (If it were a callback with another actor, on the other hand, you probably would be expected to kiss your partner.) With punches of any kind of physical violence, you will not be expected to punch anyone, though I've seen actors punch their own palm to make an effect. If the stage directions read 'Anna cries' and if the tears come, fine. If not, then play the scene organically and make it work with your choices. If the director really insists on tears, then he'll let you know. Above all, play to camera as much as possible even when it doesn't make scenic 'sense' to do so

Can I move around in front of camera?

Yes. You're not a caged lion. It's professional to ask the size of the frame so you know how to calibrate your movement. If it's a close-up, then focus performance in the face and eyes, mindful not to pop out of frame. Bobbing from side to side will make viewers seasick. You may also choose to walk into frame or perform some simple blocking but if so, let the camera operator know, so he can follow you.

You won't be expected to do the more demanding actions, unless it's a stunt audition. When I was auditioning stuntmen for *Running Scared*, for example, they all came in and checked the strength of the wall before they threw themselves onto it. If you're on a horse, don't feel the need to simulate the movement of a horse. We get it that you're on a horse.

Can I use props in a casting?

When you're battling aliens in outer space, don't forget your weapons! You can use props, as long as they don't upstage your performance. We want to be looking at you, not your toy soldier set. A mobile phone works brilliantly as a compass, a phaser gun, and a walkie talkie. The most successful props are simple things that will support your performance. Even your script can become a doctor's clipboard, and your umbrella a sword. Most casting directors will not object to whatever props might enhance your performance. Sometimes props will be provided.

Some casting directors prefer miming since it eliminates the awkwardness of props, but miming can be uncomfortable. During auditions for *Everything is Illuminated*, director Liev Schreiber said, 'I don't want actors to act with anything that's not there.' I assume that as an actor Liev hated to audition with mimed actions himself.

What if the person I'm reading with stinks?

They probably will stink. Your reader might be the casting director, who thinks she can act, but actually can't, or it may be a bored assistant. Even if it's an actor, they may not give you the energy you want. You are responsible for your performance, regardless of what you get on the other side.

Famous acting coach, Sanford Meisner, a disciple of Stanislavski, developed a technique, based on honest emotional reactions. This training is very effective and many actors boast (rightfully) that they are 'Meisner trained'. This technique can go pear-shaped in the audition room, however. I believe that this is because the spontaneous repetition exercises that Meisner employs assume that the other actor in the scene will provide emotion, or energy. You might end up reading with a corpse or a robot, which could stimulate a reaction but maybe not the one appropriate for the scene. Therefore the actor must be prepared to draw upon his own inspiration.

Can I physically interact with the casting director?

Don't expect a casting director or the reader to give you physical interaction. (It could happen but let it be on their terms, not yours.) Find your own motivation. During *Solomon Kane* castings, one actor was auditioning for the role of a prisoner who was being roughed up by Kane. I read the line with her and after an uninspired reading she said, 'I expected more physical contact from you.' Don't expect anything from us. It's your job to create the circumstances, not ours. This may well be the case on set as well.

Can I expect to do more than one take?

You may only get one take, so this is why it's crucial to enter prepared, and warmed up. If you are only offered one take, feel free to ask for another one. They might say no, but they won't knock you sideways for asking. When you do the second take, ask if they want you try something different. I recommend that you come prepared with at least two different choices, in case you do get another chance. Then the director will see your range. They may possibly be testing to see how consistent you are too, so that's why it's good to ask. The caster may ask you to do it again, and give you some direction or she may say, 'Let's play with it.'

What if I'm wrong for the role, should I audition anyway?

Yes, absolutely. It's a meeting with a casting director. If you're not right for this role, she'll remember you for another one. Whatever you do, don't decide that you're wrong for the role before you get to your meeting. Let us do that. If you believe you're wrong for the role, then you've already lost it. If you were invited, then obviously someone thinks you're right for it. Stay open, and realize that they might want to cast against type.

Dustin Hoffman didn't want to play Benjamin Braddock in *The Graduate* because he insisted that he wasn't right. He called it 'the biggest miscasting mistake anyone could make . . . this is a mark of a great director.'

What if the character is totally alien to me?

Find a way to connect with the character. What does the character want that is like what you want? Robert Carlyle is one of the most pleasant actors I've worked with. He played Hitler in CBS's *Hitler: The Rise of Evil*. His off screen personality is about as similar to Adolf Hitler as Godzilla is to Bugs Bunny. How did he pull off the role of one of history's most horrific villains? He found a way to connect with the role. 'Hitler's mother died when he was young, just as mine did,' said Carlyle. He didn't play Hitler like a monster. Hitler didn't think he was a monster after all. He played him like a petulant child.

I get so nervous. What can I do?

'If you're nervous it means you care,' said Sarah Jessica Parker. Nerves are your allies. Nerves give us energy, enthusiasm and excitement. Turn the energy towards the role. Even when actors say they're nervous, it doesn't always show, so don't announce it to the auditioners.

What advice can you give ethnic actors?

Casting can be racist and I'll be the first one to admit that. I mean the word racist, however, in the sense that we have to discriminate for artistic reasons, on the basis of race, to make a story believable. We casting directors hire actors for reasons that other types of employers would get fired for. We hire people according to the way they look, which includes considerations of race, age, and ethnicity. For example, if I'm casting a child who is supposed to be the son of Ryan Gosling and Jennifer Lawrence, then that child has to be white. When I was working on *Red Tails*, George Lucas' film about the African American pilots in World War II, we obviously had to cast black men of a certain build (short) to fit the profiles of the actual Tuskadee pilots. One agent called me at the time and mentioned that she had a wonderful black actor who was from Germany and spoke perfect German. Well of course I couldn't cast him as a German soldier. Nothing would have confused the audience more than a black German soldier. So yes, we were racist in our casting, but for sound, artistic reasons.

I realize that actors from various ethnic and racial backgrounds feel at a disadvantage when it comes to casting in North America and Europe. The perception is that white actors dominate the screen, and it's true that the industry is still largely run by white men. The fact that I feature a chapter in my book about ethnicity and casting demonstrates that there is an unresolved issue. At the same time I would say that there has never been a better time in history to be an artist of colour. 'Diversity Casting' is the language that has crept into a casting director's vocabulary. Networks, producers and casting directors are prioritizing casting as many diverse ethnicities and types as possible. The Screen Actors Guild (SAG) even offers a 'diversity-in-casting' incentive to low budget film-makers. The hit American TV series, *Glee*, won a 'diversity casting award' for its inclusion of an African American, Asian and disabled characters. CSA has a special sub-committee that specifically addresses diversity in casting and how it can be improved.

The diversity committee was formed by the CSA to work with minority and disabled groups by increasing their visibility and to improve public awareness through creative casting practices – also to identify opportunities to increase awareness of diverse choices both with Talent and Casting professionals. We contact Diversity Casting execs at Studios and Networks to promote CSA support for their events and to coordinate all efforts of these companies in diverse hiring practices.
MICHAEL SANFORD, Chair of the Diversity Casting Committee, CSA

The truth is that there is a lot of work for actors of all different races. First, casting has opened up tremendously from the old studio times. In the early days of film, actors worked only if they had a contract with a studio, and it was a certain type of actor who was invited to join the club. Films from the earlier periods featured white icons, with perfect figures and teeth. In the 1950s and early 1960s, actors like Cary Grant and Doris Day could make it; white actors, painted by the make-up department, played ethnic roles. Tastes have changed and now there would be nothing tackier than seeing a white actor, with dark make-up on, playing a Native American role.

In the 1960s and 1970s we saw the emergence of leading men like Dustin Hoffman (who at one time would have played character roles only). Influenced by the auteurs of Europe, American directors started to populate their films with actors who looked like real people; actors like Al Pacino and Barbara Streisand don't seem very alternative to us now, in a time when Denzel Washington and Lucy Liu can be stars. Francis Ford Coppola collaborating with legendary casting director, Fred Roos, was one of the first American directors to cast non-actors because they looked right for the part. Coppola claims, 'I was not looking for stars. I was looking for people who would be believable to me as real Italian-Americans . . .' (Peter Biskind, *Easy Riders, Raging Bulls.*) He also assiduously chose his extras, lending *The Godfather* that realistic, earthy look. He had to fight tooth and nail with the studio to cast Pacino. The studio executives were suggesting names like Robert Redford, Warren Beatty and Ryan O'Neal to play Michael Corleone. Coppola claims that 'They told me Al was too scruffy and looked too much like a gutter rat to play a college boy.'

The trend has continued. Now when I'm casting a film that takes place in modern-day New York or London, I cast actors from all different colours of the rainbow, to reflect the real demographics of these cities.

At a casting symposium in the UK one actor, who was originally from an Arab country, asked how he could prevent himself from getting typecast.

John Hubbard answered:

Well, one thing about being typecast is that you're working. I know that it's a particular problem with Arab actors in London and they all the time get the terrorist roles and the suicide bomber roles, but when you talk to them, at least they're working non-stop.

Whenever there is a region in conflict, invariably writers will pick up these themes and screenplays will appear, about Bosnia, about Iran, etc. I told my Iranian student to embrace her ethnicity, and that her knowledge of Farsi could be a huge asset when she entered the job market.

Actors Equity has a committee called the EEO (Equal Employment Opportunity) that is devoted entirely to encouraging diversity and inclusion in the American Theatre for actors of different races, senior actors, female actors and actors with disabilities, by enforcing the equal employment opportunity provisions in all Equity contracts.

If you are an actor of colour, get involved with the Actors Equity committee or start one in your own community. Use your race and your ethnic background to market yourself in a positive way. Create and produce diversity showcases and invite casting directors. If you feel you are being cast only one way (for example, if you always play the doctor), then create your own web series or one-man play that features you playing the role that you *want* to play.

How can I find out about casting calls?

In a perfect world, your agent will do this for you, but we don't live in a perfect world. It is your job to find the work for yourself. Casting director Beatrice Kruger says, 'You have to make sure that you're visible. If you have an agent, fine, but you can do the same thing if you don't have an agent. You have to take your life in your hands.' Stay on top of what's going on. There is no one door to knock on, or one number to call with all of the possibilities neatly listed for you. It's about keeping your ear to the ground, reading the trade magazines like *Variety, The Hollywood Reporter* and *Screen International*. Online there are numerous websites such as IMDBPro.com that list studio and independent projects in pre-production. It is absolutely essential to make the investment and register with the major search engines that casting directors use. They are Breakdown Services in the US,

Spotlight in the UK, E-TALENTA in Europe, and Showcast and IACD in Australia. Follow these sites and casting directors on social media platforms as discussed in the marketing section of this book.

When you put yourself up for a project, make sure that you know the breakdown and that there is a role appropriate for you. Casting directors are project-oriented, not actor-oriented. When I am absolutely obsessed with finding African centaurs for *Prince Caspian*, I ignore submissions from Swedish female actors that land on my desk.

When film isn't happening, turn to theatre.

If I want a film career, will I ruin it by doing commercials?

I once moderated a casting symposium when I asked the panelists to give advice to young actors at the start of their careers. One casting director said, 'Do commercials', and a director said, 'Don't do commercials.' Once again, it's not simple, and there are no rules. From a financial point of view alone, it is absurd to turn down an opportunity that could possibly pay your entire college debt, not to mention the fact that a commercial will get you exposure. Actors have even signed with top agents and managers as a result of commercial work.

There is a risk that you could get too much exposure on a particular ad that will make casters unable to see you in a serious role. If you are doing commercials, make sure that you keep your 'commercial package' separate from your 'film acting package'.

Actors who send composites (like at a modelling agency) rather than a headshot will not be taken seriously for a film role. Actors who groom themselves to nurture a more 'commercial' look, might be too 'modelly' looking to play a 'real person' for film.

This is where good management is instrumental. Manager Lainie Sorkin of Management 360 in LA nurtured actor Orlando Jones' career by booking a 7-Up commercial spot for him in which he created and played a fun character. This move succeeded in bringing in more interesting film work for him.

> But don't knock commercials for yourself. You learn a lot . . . how to
> work fast, hit your mark and learn your lines.
>
> JOHN HUBBARD

Questions to ask about the commercials

- What is the product? Do you want to be identified as the
  toilet bowl man for many years to come?

- Who are the creatives? Michael Bay, Spike Jones and
  Oliver Stone all direct commercials. Landing a commercial
  with one of them, or even being seen by them in a
  callback could start a valuable relationship.

- How long does the commercial air and in what medias?
  TV? Print? Radio?

- Where does the commercial air? If you're an American
  actor, maybe it's OK to be the toilet bowl man in Japan,
  for example.

- How much is the buy-out, in what countries, and for how
  long?

- Keep track of when and how often the ad appears. I have
  heard too many horror stories about productions and even
  agents who pocketed the money when an ad re-appeared
  beyond the terms of the buy-out.

When auditioning for a commercial, most of the same rules apply as
for film or TV casting. Make specific choices, know your type, be
yourself and keep open to play. Improvisation is a particularly useful
skill in commercial auditions. The difference between a commercial
and a film casting is that the ultimate goal is to sell a product. Know
the product that you're selling, and the specific ad campaign. For
example:

Product: Apple,
Campaign: iThink therefore iMac.

What if I can't do what the director asks, or I get poor direction at an audition?

George Lucas was known to scream, 'OK. Same thing only better,' while directing *Star Wars*. I believe that actors very often get poor direction in auditions, either from the casting director, or the director himself. Casting directors come from a variety of backgrounds, not all of them 'actor oriented'. Successful directors might come from editing, writing and even stunts or special effects, so the chances are very good that they don't understand actors. Translate their directions into actor language. Find a playable action, even if you're not given one. If a director gives you a strange direction like, 'I want her funkier', then figure out how you can turn that into an action. One time a student in my class was acting a scene in which he was trying (too hard) to play a crazy guy. He was playing an adjective ('crazy') rather than an action. I told him to imagine that there were snakes coming out of the other actor's head. Once he did that, and made the image real for him, we all believed that he was crazy. Give yourself a direction that is something you can play.

Some directors simply don't consider it their job to give direction or praise if the actor does well. Sometimes, no notes are good notes. Other directors give good playable directions. I observed Duane Clark in a callback for the TV series *The Philanthropist*. We were casting a guest star character named Bejan who was described as an extremely dangerous mafia leader. A less astute director might have told the actors to 'play him more dangerously'. Well, how do you play 'dangerous'? Duane instructed the actors to 'intensely study the other character'. This was something actors could instantly play and it produced the desired effect. If the director isn't clever enough to give playable actions, you have to think for him.

How can I find out what the director wants before the casting?

You can't know for sure, and sometimes it's hopeless because they don't even know what they want until they see it. When actors read at the auditions, it is often the first time directors hear the words of the script coming to life. It's a learning curve for them. 'The character forms in the casting,' says director John Strickland. 'It's the role made flesh.' Concentrate on what you can bring and your choices. Research the project so you arrive with an informed point of view.

Can I get cast from a show reel?

Yes, I have seen actors get cast only from show reels so it's advantageous to have a good one. Other times, the director isn't interested in looking at reels and only wants to meet actors. Generally it's an excellent screening device if the actor is far away or if we only know his work from stage.

What if I'm bombing the audition?

Ethan Hawke noted that 'the beauty of film acting is cultivating accidents and spontaneity'. Mistakes and accidents offer opportunities for actors. One of the most memorable scenes in film history was in *Midnight Cowboy* when Dustin Hoffman's character almost walks into a taxi and yells at the taxi driver, 'I'm walking here!' This was an accident. The taxi driver was not supposed to cross through the set at that time. If the casting director's phone rings during the casting, try playing it in the scene. Or use the frustration you feel when you go up on a line to invest it into the character.

What can I do to push the job through after the meeting?

You can send a postcard with your headshot on it to the casting director, thanking him for considering you or ping him on Twitter or Facebook, 'Thanks for the nice opportunity today.' Then you've reminded him of your interest in a professional way. Maybe if it's a choice between you and one other actor, and they're undecided, your courtesy will make the difference. Generally, however, there's not a flicking thing you can do once you've left the room.

Actors seem to delight in making themselves crazy. 'On that third take we did and you asked me to internalize the second speech more, did I do it? I think I understand now what you were asking. Can I try again?' This was a text message I received from an actor over the weekend after a casting. Can you say 'obsession'? When you leave the room, let it go.

I've witnessed actors who arrive saying 'I'm so embarrassed about last time. I'm so sorry.' I don't have the slightest idea what they're talking about. That means either (1) they didn't do so poorly, or (2) it has simply disappeared from my mind since it wasn't so important for me. For casters, it is usually only good or odd performances that really stand out over time.

Obsessing over the role after the audition won't affect the outcome and you will only tie yourself into knots. Try not to invest too much hope, emotion, or importance to each audition. Remember that there will always be more. If your entire well-being, either emotionally or financially, is caught up with one particular job, that desperation will read and it is likely to inhibit your chances.

How can I get feedback after an audition?

You can't. Don't expect it. I would suggest that you don't ask for it. It puts the casting director on the spot, and you might not like the answer. The truth is sometimes unhelpful and hurtful, when they are willing to say it. Often, I can't even give feedback because the director won't share his thoughts. Actors don't get cast for silly reasons and knowing the reason might be counter-productive for you. It matters little what one director thinks of you. Gene Hackman was nominated 'least likely to succeed' before he was kicked out of acting school. I'm glad he didn't listen to the opinion of the school's director. Allow yourself to harbour the thought that you were brilliant, but the role just isn't right for you, and move on.

When can I expect to be contacted about a role after the casting?

This varies widely. On some projects, I'm meeting actors months before shooting begins. TV projects on the other hand, often turn over very quickly. Sometimes no news is bad news and other times no news is no news. I've put an actor on tape in October for a role that shoots in March, and I get the approval to cast them three days before shooting. Stay in touch with the production, via your agent, about conflict dates, etc. (for example, if you get hired on another job which will disqualify you) and otherwise get on with your life.

Should I sleep with the casting director?

You can but it won't matter. Even if the casting director loves you, she is not ultimately the one who decides who plays the role. Since it's usually several people who compose the team who decides – by the time you've figured out who they are, and slept with all them, they've probably already cast the role. Stay away from the casting couch.

27

Frequently asked questions about casting directors, agents and managers

What's the difference between an agent and a casting director?

An agent works for the actor and the casting director works for production. It's the difference between buying (casting director) and selling (agent). These people should be separate. If your agent is also the casting director, then he is a servant of two masters, and you might lose out since the production is the more powerful master. In smaller cities it can happen that an agent will cast a film. In larger cities where the industry is more developed this practice is not considered professional. The Casting Society of America, the UK Casting Directors Guild and the International Network of Casting Directors bar casting directors who are agents or managers.

How can I make contact with a casting director?

Most casting directors prefer to meet actors in the context of a specific project that they are casting. Exceptionally they will have a 'general meeting' if the actor is new, or visiting the casting director's city, or introduced by an agent.

Although the 'correct' way for an actor to be introduced is via an agent, it is not unusual for actors to send material directly to casting directors. I would recommend contacting the casting director when she has a project that you may be right for. How do you know your material won't be thrown in the bin? You don't, but one way to help prevent that is by enclosing a self-addressed, stamped envelope (SASE). Never ask for material to be returned to you without an SASE.

When is a good time to call a casting director? Never. I would suggest never calling. There's too great a chance that you'll catch them in the middle of a stressful project or inopportune moment. Writing gives the recipient time to consider. Cover your bases by both emailing and posting hard copies. Be efficient and effective when communicating with casting directors. Ask yourself who you are contacting and why. Don't write a long sprawling cover letter (that won't be read). Write a concise letter getting right to the point of why you're appropriate for their casting pool. For example:

Dear Nancy Bishop,

I see that you're casting *Karate Story 3*. I'm an experienced actor, with a black belt in karate. I also speak passable Chinese. Please find my photo and CV.

Thanks for your consideration.

Lon Chu

If I'm looking specifically for karate guys, this actor will be called in. Research the project before you blindly send out your material. Think about your resources and costs. Hone in on the specific casting directors who are casting projects for which you are appropriate, rather than just sending your details out to every caster that you can find. Casting directors are seeking specific actors for specific roles.

If you randomly stop by at a casting director's office, you might get lucky and be able to say hello to her, but you also risk putting her on the spot if she is very busy. We don't like to feel rude. This is why social media is offering new opportunities to build these bridges. (See the social media marketing section.)

> We did *Tea with Mussolini* six or eight years ago now. [But recently] he phoned me up and he asked me about, 'that boy we met in the hotel'. And I thought 'OOOKAAAY!' And he was right. We met two boys in a hotel. I'd forgotten. Luckily I had the lists and I could find them. He didn't remember the name, but he did remember the essence of the boy. The reason I could find the boy he was talking about is because (a) I had the list; and (b) I could recognize the wallpaper on the tape behind him. So six years after an actual casting, Zeffirelli considered the actor in another film.
>
> the late EMMA STYLE, casting director

Is it a good idea to meet casting directors at workshops?

Many casting directors work as educators as well, including *moi* of course. We work in actor training because we want to see the talent level rise. We want an opportunity to guide and advise actors because we don't always have the time to do so in the actual casting room.

There has been some dispute about the practice of casters teaching classes. This is because scam artists have taken advantage of beginning actors, naïve about the business, taken their money, and led them down the primrose path. To address these concerns, CSA drafted guidelines in 2010 that protect both casters and actors. The main point is that actors should never be in a situation in which they are paying to audition. So if you are taking a workshop with a casting director, you may politely inquire if she is following CSA guidelines. Understand that you should be taking the class for instructional purposes, though contact with the Casting Director is certainly a nice perk of the session. Taking part in the workshop is no guarantee of employment, and casting directors are mandated to use sides from previous projects, not current ones, so that there is not confusion about the difference between the class and an audition.

If I participate in a casting director's workshop, will I get hired by that casting director?

It's possible. Actors have been discovered in workshops. I do cast actors from my own classes, but usually not immediately. Like many things, it's about timing. If I am looking for a specific type on a project and that person shows up in my class . . . then, yes! But sometimes I am teaching when casting work is slow, so then I encourage actors to stay in touch and naturally I will consider them later when a role comes up for them. Taking a class with a casting director is certainly no guarantee of employment, so you participate in the spirit of learning and making connections. I know for sure that actors who have met each other in my classes form networks, help each other, and host each other in their respective cities. Actors have been 'discovered' in workshops too, like Oscar Isaac:

> Actor Oscar Isaac (*Inside Llewyn Davis*) started his career in Florida. He took a two-day workshop with Lori Wyman, a Miami casting director, early on in his career. Lori then brought him in to read for *BIG TROUBLE*, directed by Barry Sonnenfeld. Barry cast Oscar when Lori told him that Oscar had just been accepted to Juilliard.
>   LORI WYMAN, casting director, Miami

How do I find an agent?

Work and be visible. Make your own projects, when you're not getting offers. Do showcases, and take classes. If you're doing good theatre work, or training in a quality program, you will attract the attention of an agent. Simply sending your photo and resumé to every agency you can find is not the way. Good agencies get hundreds of these blind solicitations every day. An actor once asked me: 'How can I make an agent watch my show reel?' Of course you can't guarantee that your material will even be opened. That's why it's advisable to target specific agents with specific requests. Invite agents to a project, and attach reviews of your work. Instead of sending a huge envelope that has to be opened with thousands of pictures, send a postcard with one image, and a succinct message with a website address on the back. Keep cards with photos in your wallet in case you run into a good contact during the course of your day. See Chapter 19 on social media for more hints.

Research the agencies that are available to you, and identify a good match. Everyone wants to be represented by the A-list agencies, but if you're at the beginning of your career you may have to work your way up. Research also means networking, which includes asking actors, teachers, casting directors and other industry professionals for agent recommendations. IMDbPro provides a list of agencies, with their respective Star-Meter rankings. The lower the agency ranking, the more star names they represent. In the US, Breakdown Services and the *Ross Reports* list agencies. In the UK, look at the *Actors and Performers Yearbook* or Spotlight's *Contacts*. Gauge each agency's clientele and whether or not you fit. In addition to considering the calibre of actor they represent, examine what types sit on their roster. Would you complement or compete with their other clients? Some agencies specialize in particular types; The Willow agency in London represents little people, for example. In most cases, you'll be looking for a local agent. Unless you're a star, it is unlikely that a London, New York or LA agent will accept an actor living elsewhere.

Take the trouble to learn the agency's submission policies. Some agencies categorically reject submissions without an industry referral. That means you need a recommendation from someone they trust. Ask a director or producer you've worked with if you can use their name when contacting an agent. Personal contacts or friends registered in the same agency could help as well.

Watch out for scams. It is normal and expected that agents will take a percentage of your salary. This is how they make their living. In most cases, the percentage should be no more than 10 or 15%. If it's a SAG (Screen Actors Guild) contract, this fee is often taken off the top of your salary (i.e. production adds 10% for the agent). If it is a non-SAG contract, expect them to take a bite out of your wages. Check this before you sign on the dotted line.

Any reputable North American or British agent will not charge a fee to accept you. I have heard reports of so-called 'agents' who charge a fee for administration, photos and website entry, or insist that clients attend expensive in-house training. These are not agents but scam artists. An agent's job is to promote you, find you work, and *then* take a commission (not before). Talk to other registered actors before you sign. To investigate the legitimacy of a US agency, check the ATA (Association of Talent Agents) website to see if they're registered. Agents with SAG and Equity associations are also held to professional standards.

> It's the agent's job to get actors considered . . . then it's up to the actor to win it.
>
> JEREMY CONWAY, Conway VanGelder, Grant, London

Above all, remember that even once you've signed with an agent, self-promotion and networking continue. Don't expect an agent to solve all of your problems. An agent can get you a more effective contract, more money, a better dressing room, etc., but they can't get the work for you.

What is the difference between an agent and manager? Do I need both?

A personal manager is engaged in the occupation of advising and counseling talent and personalities in the entertainment industry. Personal managers have the expertise to find and develop new talent and create opportunities for those artists which they represent. Personal managers act as liaison between their clients and agents, others in the entertainment industry, and the general public.

The National Conference of Personal
Managers website

Managers are more common in the United States, than in the UK and Europe. In Los Angeles and New York many actors do have both an agent and a manager because actors need all the support they can get in such competitive markets.

The agent actively procures work for an actor, while the manager is meant to work cooperatively with the agent to manage the process. Legally speaking, managers are not allowed to find work for their clients, though almost all of them do. Managers take on actors who they believe in, and view their relationship as a long term collaboration. Managers typically sign three-year contracts while for agents a one-year contract is common. The great advantage is that managers concentrate on a smaller number of clients than an agent. While agencies might promote packages of actors, a manager takes time to promote you as an individual artist.

> We as a breed have an overview. That's one of the key things that differentiates us from agents. Agents by definition have larger lists of people they work with. On a daily basis I work with eight or ten people. A good manager is a very handy person to have on your side.
>
> DEREK POWER, Manager

Tammy Rosen (who manages Michael Sheen among many others), a manager at Sanders, Armstrong and Caserta Management, notes that 'a large agency may have a five minute phone call to promote ten actors, but a manager will use that same five minutes to promote one actor'.

In exchange for their focused attention, managers may in turn extract a higher commission than an agent, taking as much as 15–20% of your salary. This would be in addition to your agency's fee. Clarify this with a manager from the start. The TMA (Talent Managers Association) and the NCOPM (National Conference of Personal Managers) ensure that managers maintain professional and ethical practices.

Brad Pitt has a manager but so does Wendy Wannarole who is at the beginning of her career. How a manager works with a star is different from how she will work with a less matured talent. Rosen uses the metaphor of a company to describe how the manager works with someone like Brad Pitt; 'The way I see it is the actor is the owner of the company and the manager is the president of the board of directors. The board is composed of the agent, the publicist, the make-up artist, and the lawyer, etc.' The manager manages this team. Ideally the manager is in a position to nurture the actor, specifically guiding not only his career choices, but also his image, and his relationships with specific producers, casting directors and industry professionals. The manager could go out on a limb specifically spinning the client for a particular role.

In the case of Wendy Wannarole, the manager may be the one who actually positions her with a prestigious agency. 'An agent might say to a manager for example, "Let me know when she's viable. Show me something that will make her more interesting than the other clients in my agency",' explains Rosen. Lesser-known actors get lost in larger agencies, which is why a manager is pivotal. The manager is also more likely to handle a complicated transaction, like getting a foreign actor an O–1 visa for example. Many European actors land a manager before an agent for that reason.

Associates and assistants

Learn the names of the people who answer the phones and monitor the reception rooms. They could be your greatest allies. Our assistants report to us about actors who were rude and pushy in the waiting room. We also respect our assistants' opinions and, yes, they can make suggestions about whom we see. It goes without saying that actors, like all people on the planet, should be kind and courteous to everyone, but especially to assistants, who may become associates and eventually casting directors themselves.

What's a casting agent?

There is no such thing as a 'casting agent', If you want to really irritate a casting director, call her a casting agent. My friends learned this and now they do it all the time. The official position of the Casting Society of America is:

> Although the term 'Casting Agent' is frequently used incorrectly by those outside the business and in the media, it is not accurate. An Agent is defined as 'a person or business authorized to act on another's behalf.' In the Entertainment Industry a Talent Agent procures jobs and negotiates deals for the actor. For this service they receive a fee usually based on a percentage of the actor's wages.
>
> Casting Directors are hired by studios, networks or production companies and are employed to select actors for consideration. Casting Directors also negotiate, on behalf of those companies, the deals to hire the actors selected. Casting Directors and Casting Associates do not represent actors or receive any fees from the actors they present for hire.

PART SIX

Practical exercises

Your camera and you

A camera is a necessary investment for anyone interested in screen acting. For those who were taught the inside-out method of acting, watching the performance from the outside can be off-putting and painful. In *An Actor Prepares*, Stanislavski warned his students: 'You must be very careful in the use of a mirror. It teaches an actor to watch the outside rather than the inside of a role.' In the beginning stages of learning film acting, however, I believe that actors must get to know themselves on screen. It's necessary to see when an eyebrow goes astray, or to realize when one is bouncing out of frame. In front of camera, actors can rehearse auditions, and practise the techniques of screen acting. The camera is essential for discovering that middle ground that balances the artist between overacting and dead face. We talk about naturalism but honestly there is nothing natural about acting on stage or on camera. In this section I suggest exercises for use in class or on your own.

While these exercises are helpful for the process of learning screen acting, it is ultimately important, however, not to become self-obsessed. When filming, you need an outside person, like a director, to direct your performance and ensure that your work fits with the whole. In a production situation, trust the director. Directors will not stand for actors who run to the monitor after each shot, and demand a re-take if they're not satisfied.

Exercise 1. Pre-casting warm-up

What do you do before you go on stage, or on camera? For every actor it's different. Some actors jump up and down, some sing, and some do yoga. Figure out what YOU need to do for yourself in order to perform well. In acting classes, the class warms up. At an audition no one will warm you up and you may only get one take so you have to be 'warm' from the get go. The problem is . . . do you feel comfortable warming up in the reception room before the audition? Probably not. Here's an exercise to be done in a chair, based on the teachings of Alexander.

Frederick Alexander (1869–1955) was an actor, who developed a system of physical exercises to alleviate tension. His technique was based on the theory that stress in the body can inhibit the flow of emotions. Actors tend to push to manipulate a performance, creating tension in the body. Stress can be channelled; the actor's creativity comes in the way he reacts to and manages that stress. If an actor holds tension in his neck, for example, it will constrict the voice. These are the actor's reactions, not the characters. Therefore, the actor must be in a relaxed state in order to perform well. The Alexander Technique teaches actors a way to organize, be aware of and manage body tension, directing it towards character not towards interference with performance.

You can practise this relaxation exercise in a chair, without making an ass of yourself in the reception room.

- Place your feet flat on the floor.

- Ensure that you are well balanced on your sitting bones.

- Sit on the edge of chair.

- Concentrate on breathing deeply.

- Concentrate on lengthening the spine in two directions.

- Visualize your head posed at the top of your spine.

- Visualize your torso lengthened and widened.

- Concentrate internally on this mantra:

    Let my neck be free, to let my head go forward and up, to let my torso lengthen and widen, to let my legs release away from my torso and let my shoulders widen.

Imagine a ball of energy moving from your toes to your ankles, to your shins, thighs and buttocks. Visualize the energy moving through each part of your body, including the torso, the hips, and all of your joints. Include your neck, shoulders and facial muscles. Relaxing the jaw and throat is important for vocal freedom.

Once you have isolated each body part through relaxation, gradually allow each vertebrate in your back to collapse, with the head leading the torso into a forward bend. Your torso moves as a unit from the hip sockets.

Then allow your head to lead your torso up so that you are vertical again.

Clear your mind, take a breath, and concentrate on the choices you have made for the character. Run the lines in your head. Step in for your audition.

> Turkish casting director, Harika Ujgar, advises her actors to meditate every day. 'How can you create a character when you're not connected to yourself?', she asks. The character comes from inside. Meditation encourages actors to connect with the breath, and the creative flow. How can you act if you're not breathing? How to do a good audition? Connect with the breath!

Exercise 2. Telling a story

- Work in pairs, off camera. Choose a theme and think of a particular moment in your life. Themes could include:

  - something very embarrassing;

  - a time when you got caught;

  - something that happened to you when you were a child that changed your life.

- Tell your partner the story.

- Listen carefully and empathetically to your partner's story, memorizing each detail.

- Now work on camera. The partner tells her partner's story, in first person to the camera.

- She may change a few details to make the scene work.

- Evaluate.

This exercise encapsulates what acting is. You're telling someone else's story, as if it were your own. This scene should reflect you, and your personality. Were you able to convincingly and naturally tell your partner's story? Did we believe that it was your story? Was it a natural performance?

Exercise 3. Blank scenes

I call these scenes 'blank' because the actor needs to fill in the blanks; we know nothing about the characters, who they are, where they are, or what their motives are. Famous Russian actor and teacher, Michael Chekhov, devised blank scenes such as these for his technique, so they are sometimes called 'Chekhovian'. I use them in my casting workshops because they are excellent exercises to practise making choices. Practising a blank scene is not unlike doing an audition for a film. Often you haven't read the script and know very little about the character so you have to make choices. Practise these scenes with a partner. Make specific choices, based on answering the following questions.

- Who am I?
- Where am I?
- Who am I talking to?
- What do I want?
- What are the stakes?
- Where are the changes?

Blank scene I

A: I didn't say that.

B: You did. I heard you.

A: It doesn't matter. You can't prove it.

B: Everyone heard you.

A: You're funny. You're really funny.

B: You're saying that . . .

A: That you're funny.

B: That I'm funny.

A: Hilarious.

B: There is nothing funny about this.

A: Everything is funny about this.

B: We all know you said it.

A: I repeat. I didn't say it.

B: You said it.

Blank scene II

A: Hey, haven't I seen you before?

B: I don't think so.

A: I'm sure I did. I saw you at . . .

B: I'm new here.

A: Perhaps you only look like . . .

B: That must be it. I have one of those faces.

A: Those faces meaning . . .

B: Meaning I look like a lot of people.

A: I was thinking actually that you look like my cousin.

B: Wait, maybe we have seen each other before.

A: Yes, I'm sure we have. It was at . . .

B: It was last year perhaps?

A: It was more recently, I believe.

B: I need to go.

The possibilities are endless for these scenes. Experiment with playing each scene three different ways, as you would during the casting. As a warm up, play off camera with your partner. Then take turns in front of camera. You will have to agree what the relationship is between you and decide where you are. You don't have to share your objective; that can be secret.

Then ask your partner to read off-screen in a neutral voice, giving no energy (as you might get at a casting), and focus the camera on your face. Rise to the challenge of making specific, actable choices without getting inspiration or energy from the other actor.

Exercise 4. Listening and the inner monologue

In front of camera, listening and reacting can be even more important than speaking. When I'm casting a supporting role, with few lines, it's often hard to find dialogue where the character speaks several lines consecutively. So I keep the camera on the actor while I speak all of the other lines. These types of roles present an even bigger challenge to actors than a character who speaks all the time. The actor has to be constantly on, engaged in an ongoing inner monologue, or soundtrack of thoughts, listening and reacting to all of the actions and speech of the characters around him.

I like to challenge actors by giving them scenes with few lines, because it shows the director that the actor has the skill to be featured in a reaction shot. On a TV set there may be five cameras shooting at the same time, catching every character's reaction. If your reactions and listening skills are not up to par, you'll get less screen time. Michael Caine, in *Acting in Film*, discusses how surprised he was when he started working in Hollywood with actors like Sylvester Stallone, who wanted to cut their own lines. Caine came from a theatre background where everyone wanted as many lines as possible. It was because Stallone realized that the most interesting moments are in the silences, not in the speech.

The following exercises, to be done in pairs, or in a classroom, are designed to develop the listening and inner monologue skills that are imperative in an audition as well as on set. In castings, so often actors throw away their silences and reactions by reading the other character's lines instead of listening. When an actor reads the lines, we only see their eyelids and the top of their head.

Take 1. Medium shot

Actor B stands off camera and tells a story (see the example below). The camera shoots Actor A who is listening in a medium frame. The featured actor does not speak, but merely listens and reacts silently. It is best to choose a story that will impact the actor who is listening. Here's an example: Actor A (the featured, listening actor) should be female and Actor B is male. The set-up for the scene is that B has invited A to meet at a café. They are a couple who have not been dating long. B is there to tell A that she is pregnant. Actor B improvises a one-minute-long monologue in which she explains the situation. Actor A has the camera on him and he will react in the moment to what she is saying. The pregnancy is a good example because he can choose a variety of responses.

Take 2. The 'less is more' theory

Shoot in close-up. This time Actor B can tell the same story, or a different story (something that impacts Actor A). Actor A will listen again, being mindful of the fact that this is a close-up. In my class, I ask how the acting changes in a close-up shot. The class will often answer that less is more, and that the acting should be smaller. The camera is right there, so it will pick up everything. Thinking is enough for the camera. So in Take 2, Actor A will go with the theory that less is more, and keep his reactions contained, and smaller than in life.

Take 3. The 'more is more' theory

Shoot in close-up again, and Actor B will tell the same story. In a close-up, the actor loses the ability to communicate through body language. The actor becomes a floating head in space. Therefore, the face and the eyes become the only instruments of communication. Therefore, some actors practise a more intense facial reaction in close-up. Sometimes the actor has to listen more loudly than he would in real life. This means that, contrary to the last experiment, the reactions might actually be bigger than in life.

Take 4. The 'harbour a secret' theory

Keep the camera in close-up. This time, as Actor A is listening to Actor B's story, he will concentrate on playing contrast in his inner monologue. How to play contrast? There are times when someone tells us something and we don't want them to know how we feel. This can be achieved when Actor A has a secret. Imagine a poker game. Keeping a secret is an effective choice because often we want to keep our cards close to our chest. For example, he could choose that he's upset about the pregnancy because he is already married with children, but he doesn't want his girlfriend to know this.

Evaluate

After going through these four takes, watch the tape, and evaluate your performance.

Which take was the most effective? When you're evaluating yourself and each other, ask the following questions.

Take 1

- Were you really listening?

- Did it *look like* you were really listening?

- If you were the director, would you want to feature this actor in a reaction shot?

The first take is probably the easiest in terms of really listening because you've never heard Actor B's story before, but is really listening interesting to watch on camera? Sometimes our faces are blank when we're listening. This could be OK, if the character is deliberately playing a poker face. Or it may be boring. You might have to consider other techniques.

Take 2

- Is it effective to contain your expressions and reactions?
- Does this create a believable performance?
- If you were a director, would you want to feature this actor in close-up?
- Is it under-played? Is it over-played?

Some people naturally have expressive faces, and large reactions. If you are one of these people, then you may well have to concentrate on limiting your facial expressions, and learn to develop stillness, keeping the reactions and inner monologue in the eyes and not in the face. Some unconsciously direct their responses into an overly scrunched forehead. (I have heard of acting teachers who suggest putting masking tape on the forehead to break the habit.) Beginning actors invariably think that film acting is about doing nothing. Doing nothing, however, often results in that anathematizing dead face. Watch out for it.

Take 3

- Was the face alive?
- Was the performance interesting and engaging? Was the screen filled with information?
- If you were a director, would you want to feature this actor?
- Was the performance too over the top or at the right level?
- Was it interesting? Could we see the character's specific thoughts?

What actors learn from this exercise is that they can get away with a lot more than they think they can. Theatre actors come with the impression that film acting is 'smaller' or less exaggerated than theatre acting, so they're terrified of overacting, and they end up with a performance that is frankly boring and flat on screen. Other actors may watch Take 3 and realize that for them, less *is* more. For actors who are naturally animated, reacting more intensively in the face might cause them to jump out of the screen. Actors new to film acting need to experience this process of experimentation to learn what level is right for them.

Take 4

- Did the actor play contrast in his reactions?
- Was the screen filled with information?
- Was this performance more effective than the previous takes?
- Was keeping a secret effective?

The camera loves contrast, and variety. The camera also loves mystery and secrets. An actor who has an active and complex inner monologue is likely to have the most compelling performance. When you have a long reaction shot, the worst thing you can do is to react in only one way. Keep the thoughts spinning, active, varied and specific.

Exercise 5. 'Over there'

This exercise draws from Commedia Dell'Arte techniques originated by Tim Robbins' theatre company, the Actors' Gang. This exercise is intended to help actors practise and develop their ability to communicate feelings through the eyes. The Actors' Gang, inspired by the teaching of George Bigot of Cirque du Soleil, developed a style based on the actor being 'stated' in one of the four primary emotions: sadness, anger, happiness, or fear. That means that the actor finds inspiration that will crank him into an optimum high intensity of emotion. On a scale from 1 to 10, the actor plays a 10. He then brings that emotion with him to play objectives in the scene.

In this style of theatre, the actor must be heightened in one of these emotional states at all times and send it out through the eyes, making contact with the audience. I adapted this approach to a film acting exercise called 'Over there'. In film you can't connect with the audience, so you have to connect with an image near the camera lens.

Set up the camera and mark a spot next to it *at eye level.* The actor steps in front of camera, points at the spot and says, 'Over there'. She does this four times, once each for the four emotions listed above. The first time she is pointing to something that is deeply sad. She must imagine the saddest thing in the world to her, her dead child, or burned down home, etc. The second time it will be something that makes her incredibly happy like her soldier husband, thought dead, returning home safely. The actor continues through this process, pointing to something that makes her angry, then something that prompts fear.

Evaluate

Watch the tape, and evaluate:

- Was the actor in a heightened state of emotion? If you were measuring on a scale of 1 to 10, was she all the way at a 10?

- Did the actor communicate clearly with her eyes?

- Was it interesting to watch and was it effective?

- What does the actor need to work on to improve communicating with the eyes?

I realize that there is a contradiction in this exercise. I have spent a whole book emphasizing the point that actors need to play action, not emotion. Now here's an exercise that is all about playing emotion. This 'stated' sense of awareness can be applied to a scene in which there is an objective. I could see this training in Tim Robbins' performance in *War of the Worlds* in which he played a petrified home-owner cowering in his basement, while terrifying aliens invade the Earth. He was in a permanent sense of fear that riddled his eyes and body, while at the same time playing the objective to fight for survival.

Exercise 6. Improvisation/Playing the objective

The following are examples of strong objectives. Note that they all take direct objects (i.e. 'to seduce him').

- To challenge
- To convince
- To change
- To avenge
- To hurt
- To amuse
- To tease
- To undress
- To scare

- To arouse
- To irritate
- To forgive
- To scold
- To placate
- To motivate
- To punish
- To shame
- To seduce

Choose from the list above or create your own. Select an objective that is an action verb. Actors sometimes choose scenarios, or adjectives instead of doable actions.

Set the camera at eye level, and shoot three times. Actors choose three contrasting objectives to play.

Take 1. Wide shot

Choose one objective and play it to the mini-screen that is located on the right side of most cameras. As in the exercise before, play your objective with the intensity of a 10 out of 10. Drive the stakes high. Play for life and death. Speak to the mini-viewing screen as if to a scene partner, improvising your objective. Keep your awareness

that you're playing for a wide shot an
information, doing what you need to fulfil yo

Take 2. Medium shot

Choose a contrasting objective. The frame is smaller now, s
your performance to fit the screen.

Take 3. Close-up

Choose yet a different contrasting objective, but this time play it silently without speech. Be aware of the screen size, so that you don't pop out of frame. Find stillness while fighting for your goal. Play in the eyes. Be like Medusa and kill with your eyes.

NOTE: Don't worry if your objective isn't exactly clear to the audience, as long as it's clear to you. The film-maker must provide context for your objectives. When you have a purpose, that aim drives the scene, whatever the context may be.

Evaluate

Take 1

Is the actor filling the screen? Are the stakes high which drive the objective?

Take 2

Has the performance changed to adapt to screen size? Is the actor playing his objective at a 10?

Take 3

Is the actor playing in the eyes? Is the silent performance effective? Is the actor 'stated'?

...versation

gy.

...oning Actor B. Set up a
For example, A has just
A wants B (her boyfriend
ck her up. B will not come
...sed at least three different

...er. 'It's wet, I'm cold and

2 A threatens B. 'I'm g... ...ak up with you unless you come and pick me up.'

3 A bargains with B. 'I'll give you a little surprise if you come pick me up.'

Watch the performance. This is an exercise that practises playing different tactics and strategies to achieve an objective. Your character wants or needs something from the other character.

Evaluate

When evaluating the performance, ask:

- Were there three clear strategies to reach the objective?
- Were the strategies believable and persuasive?
- Was there contrast in the performance with each different strategy?

Exercise 8. 'Get out of the chair'

PHOTO 10
Photographer: Ashe Kazanjian

I'll only get out of the chair when I believe you. This is a fun exercise to do with or without camera.

Actor A's objective is to get Actor B to stand up from the chair. Actor A can use whatever tactics necessary but Actor B will not get up out of the chair until he believes him. That means that he must see truth in Actor A's eyes.

Try specific lines. Power phrases are:

I love you.

I want to kill you.

Say it. Mean it. The person sitting in the chair should not stand up until she believes him.

If you shoot it, shoot this exercise with Actor B sitting directly next to the lens and Actor A in front of camera.

Exercise 9. Sight reading techniques

Also called 'cold' reading. There are times when a casting director will throw you a text that you've never seen before. It's called sight reading or cold reading, and the best way to beat your fear of it is to practise. Remember from an earlier chapter that cold reading is what you'll be expected to do at a Woody Allen audition, when no sides are issued in advanced and no sides leave the casting area.

When I teach in Germany and France, my students insist that they always get the text in advance and they have no need of this skill, but my casting colleagues in these countries tell me it isn't so. Even the most organized of casting directors might get a script change suddenly.

Use sight reading as an opportunity to bring fresh, unbiased energy to the scene. If the caster just threw it to you, she knows that you're reading it cold.

The technique for sight reading is as follows.

For practice in partners (as an extension of the 'Chair' exercise)

Hold the text and put your thumb on the first sentence. Read it to yourself first, and once you've got it, take your eyes off the page and feed the text into the eyes of your seated partner. (If you don't have a partner, read it into that spot next to the camera lens.) When you read it out, make sure that you believe what you're saying. Your partner will look into your eyes. When he believes you, he will get out of the chair. If he doesn't believe you, he sits. Keep reading out the sentence into his eyes, until he believes you.

Then move down to the next sentence and repeat. This process slows the reading down. It will not be fast, but it will be honest. Some actors even find that their first reading is the best and afterwards, they are struggling to repeat the same freshness.

Try this exercise on Peter Morgan's monologue from the film, *360*. I have deliberately divided it up into chunks of text that you can easily manage. Don't cheat by reading it in advance.

```
MALE COLD READING MONOLOGUE

Tyler in 360
INT. State Correctional Facility

                    TYLER
          Ms. Olsen, I believe I've done
          everything you've asked of me
```

here . . . I've worked hard, tried
hard . . . but what if I'm no
different? After all the work we've
done? What if I haven't changed?

(a beat)

I know we worked on the idea of me
returning to Kentucky, to where my
parents are . . . to start a clean
slate . . .
and God knows I'm impatient to start
working again . . .
but the way I feel now, I think maybe
I should go to that half-way house
first. For my own protection.
I mean, like you said . . . I've been
in an all-male situation here for six
years, it's going to be quite a shock
being on the outside again . . . with
all the temptations and
distractions . . .
And I'd hate for everything we've
done together to be undone . . .

(a beat)

You said you'd spoken to some people
in Louisville . . . who have
experience helping people like
me . . .
They can just pick me up at
Louisville airport.
Because I don't ever want to end up
in a place like this again . . .

How did it go? Did you feel like you brought an honesty to the scene?
OK, so now that you know the monologue, you can try again but with
an informed knowledge of what's coming next. Now you can answer
the who, what, where questions, even without reading the whole
script.

- Who are you? Tyler, a sex-crimes offender.

- Where am I? A state correctional facility.

- Who am I talking to? Ms. Olsen, a social worker.

- What do I want? Freedom from prison and protection from my darker side.

- What's at stake? My freedom.

Now try it again and see how it changes. Can you manage to keep it fresh on the second reading?

```
FEMALE COLD READING MONOLOGUE
360 by Peter Morgan
INT. Denver Airport cafe

                    LAURA
          You ever been to Brazil?
          You'd like it. Everyone likes it.
          We have the best beaches in
          the world.
          That's where I live my life. The
          beach.
          Where we spent all day, after school.
          It's what drove me crazy about London
          . . . not hearing the waves . . .

               (a beat)

          It's the first thing I'm going to do
          when I get home . . . go to the beach
          . . . lie down, close my eyes . . .
          and smoke a joint.
          I'd like a joint now. Wouldn't you?
          Three hundred and sixty-four days of
          the year I'm a good, Catholic girl.
          Right now I'm just feeding off the
          situation.
          The situation we're in now . . . here
          in an airport . . . a storm blowing
          outside . . . all the planes on the
          ground . . .
```

```
no one knows where we are . . . no
one can reach us . . .
the situation is crazy . . . all the
normal rules of life are turned
inside out . . .
It's perfect . . .
So . . . we have a thirty dollar credit
for food and drink . . . But we already
agreed we're not hungry, right?
So let's celebrate instead. .!
. . . or drown our sorrows. Which?
```

How did it go? Once more, did you feel like you brought a freshness to the scene? Now that you know the monologue, try it again but with an informed knowledge of what's coming next. Now you can answer the who, what, where questions, even without reading the whole script.

- Who am I? Laura, a Brazilian girl travelling back home from London.

- Where am I? The Denver Airport café during a snowstorm.

- Who am I talking to? Tyler. A strange man whom I find attractive.

- What do I want? To enjoy Tyler. Sexually? Socially? (Make a choice.)

- What is at stake? Her heart.

(Background: Laura has just left her boyfriend who was cheating on her back in London. She wants to have that first affair to see what it feels like.)

Tips for sight-reading at castings

1 Tip #1. Remember that you don't have to completely cold read if you don't feel comfortable with it. If a caster thrusts a page into your hand, ask to take it into the hall for a few moments while they see someone else, and then come back in.

2 Tip #2. Hold the script high (but not in front of your face). If the shot is in close up, we won't see the script in the shot anyway, but even if we do, so what? It's a cold read. If you hold the script low, your eyes have to go further down to find the words, and we'll just see your eyelids.

3 Tip #3. Listen and don't read the other character's lines. We need to see your reaction. That will be the most interesting part of your performance

4 Tip #4. In order to save your place on the page, as you listen, keep your thumb in the margin on the dialogue that is currently being read and keep it moving down the script as you progress.

Dyslexia: Many actors are dyslexics and they tend to be very good at memorizing lines quickly to compensate. If you are dyslexic, let the casting director know in advance so she will be sensitive about giving you a random text. In the case that you are given a cold script, feel free to ask if you can have a few moments with it.

PART SEVEN

Scene analysis

In this section, there are scenes from films on which I have collaborated. You can use these scenes for practice, either in front of the camera or to practise your written scene analysis. Normally the casting director will provide the agent with a brief plot synopsis. Other times the project is so secretive that you will know almost nothing and have to make choices, based on instincts and the information you can extract from the scene itself.

For each scene ask the following questions:

1 *Who am I?* Start with the character's basic identity. I am . . . It's okay if you don't know a great detail about the character. You can get a lot of information from the scene.

2 *Where am I?* It says this right at the top of the scene. Note whether it's interior (INT.) or exterior (EXT.) It will affect how you play the scene. Is it a public space like a restaurant or a private space like a bedroom? Are there other characters there watching you?

3 *Who am I talking to?* Establish what your relationship is with the other character. You need or want something from them. Figure out what that is and relate it to your objective.

4 *What do I want? The objective.* This is the most important question because your answer will dictate how you play the scene. Surprisingly actors often neglect to answer this basic question. If you don't want something, then you've got nothing to play. Choose an action verb that excites you.

5 *What are the stakes?* What risk is your character taking? What does your character have to lose? This gives us the urgency or the tone in the scene. Choose the highest stakes that the context allows.

6 *Where does the scene change?* The camera loves contrast and change. In any well-written scene, there is at least one transitional moment, something on which the scene hinges. Often, it's marked by a moment of discovery, when the character learns or decides something. Choose where that is

and mark it on your script. You don't have to plan *how* you'll change but know that there is a change. Here is an opportunity to play opposites. For example, if the scene is about attraction, it is also about repulsion.

7   *What are the special technical or character considerations for playing this scene in a casting?* Ask yourself, what props, if any, might help your performance. Think about the geography of the scene and where you will place off-camera characters and items to which the scene refers.

8   *What page are we on in the script?* Normally a feature-length film script is 100–120 pages. The page number tells us where we are in the story. This can be helpful when you consider the actor as story teller. Although the character isn't aware, actors should know that they are telling a story. If we're on page 11, it's the first meeting of the romantic leads. Think about where they are going. If it's page 89, it's one of those final scenes when the monster finally reveals itself to man. How desperate is the character at this point in the story?

9   *What genre is this piece?* You should have this information in advance, but when you're not sure, ask. I was casting a black comedy once, and a number of actors who came in weren't aware that it was a comedy. When the actors were missing the jokes, so were we. If it's a comedy, find the punch lines and punch them. If it's a historical drama, do some research on the period. If it's based on a comic book, read it and then don't worry about doing a long, thorough, Freudian analysis of your character. The bad guy in these films is just the bad guy. If you're a vampire, then your objective is to suck the other character's blood. Don't make it any more complicated than that.

Scene I

MIRRORS
Screenplay by: Alexandre Aja and
Gregory Levasseur

Directed by: Alexandre Aja
Studio: 20th Century Fox

Page 16, Scene 22
This horror/mystery film, starring Kiefer
Sutherland and Paula Patton, was a re-make of
an earlier Korean film, *Into the Mirror*. This
early scene establishes the characters and
their backstory.

INT. EARLY EVENING - BEDROOM HOUSE

> (Amy is not pleased to see him -
> She's beside herself with anger -)

> AMY
> What is this? I already asked you not
> to drop by without calling, didn't I?

> BEN
> You never take my calls!

> AMY
> I don't need your calls in the middle
> of the night. I'm better off without
> them.

> BEN
> I haven't had a drink in three
> months, but, then again, how would
> you know?

> AMY
> I don't want to know, Ben and I don't
> want to hear about it. It's not my
> problem. You're not my problem. Now
> please . . .

> BEN
> Wait. I got a job, OK? I'm trying to
> get back on my feet . . .
> (She doesn't want to hear it.)

                    BEN
Come on, Amy . . . You don't think
people can change?

                    AMY
God! We re not talking about people,
we're talking about you. How many
times did you tell me you were gonna
change?

                    BEN
You know very well what happened. And
I know it's not an excuse, but I
needed help.

                    AMY
. . . and instead of getting help,
you drank yourself into oblivion.
Yeah, I remember and so do the kids.

                    BEN
It's you that I needed.

                    AMY
I was here, Ben.

                    BEN
To judge me, like the others.

                    AMY
How dare you say that?! . . . When I
was the only one at the precinct who
defended you. I was the only one who
believed in you . . .

    (Ben moves closer to his ex-wife)

                    BEN
Please, you need to give us another
chance.

    (Discouraged, she smiles - How many
    other chances did she already give
                    him?)

```
                    AMY
        Look, I will never stop you from
        seeing your children but we have to
        set up some rules.

        (Out of nowhere, Ben hits the wall
                with his bare fist)

                    BEN
        WHAT RULES?! IT'S MY SON'S FUCKING
        BIRTHDAY TODAY! COME ON AMY, WHAT
        RULE IS GOING TO STOP ME FROM SEEING
        HIM?
```

Analysis for Amy

- *Who am I?* Amy Carson. Ben's estranged wife and mother of two children. She works for the police. (How do we know? She mentions the 'precinct'.)

- *Where am I?* In her bedroom. This used to be Ben's bedroom.

- *Who am I talking to?* Ben, her estranged husband.

- *What do I want?* The most obvious objective to play is that she wants him to leave, right? After all, that's what she says. But what does she really want? Does she want her husband to be an alcoholic and neglectful father? No, she wants him to be a good loving husband and father. I encourage actors who are playing this scene to play with the dynamics of the choice. Maybe there is a moment when she almost breaks and allows him to stay because she really wants her husband back. It's easy to play this scene in anger. Find the love in the scene. Try playing opposite the anger.

- *Where does the scene change?* First, she asks Ben to go away but Ben changes the playing field when he says, 'It was you that I needed.' How does this affect Amy? Does it make her angry? Guilty? We know there is a change when she smiles and wonders how many chances she's already given him. Certainly the scene changes for her when Ben hits the wall and yells at her.

- *What are the stakes?* Her children and her marriage. Certainly these are high stakes for her.

- *Technical considerations.* Play the space. They are in the privacy of the bedroom but the children are nearby. She doesn't want them to hear.

- *What page are we on?* Page 16. We are very early in the script. This scene is largely expository, communicating to the audience what took place before. The couple are at the beginning of their journey through the script.

- *Character considerations.* She is a cop, probably from a working-class background.

- *What is the genre?* The film turns into a horror/thriller. This should make no difference in the playing of the scene. This is a naturalistic family scene.

Analysis for Ben

- *Who am I?* Ben Carson. We know this much from the scene: He had a drinking problem. He lost his job as a cop, but he's got a new job now. He is separated from his wife. If we read the script, we know that he is now working as a security guard.

- *Where am I?* In the bedroom, that he once shared with his wife.

- *Who am I talking to?* Amy, his estranged wife.

- *What do I want?* He wants to be with his son to celebrate his birthday today. He wants to return to his wife and children.

- *Where does the scene change?* There are different beats for Ben. He never gives up his objective but he tries different strategies. His first strategy is 'I've changed.' Now that he's stopped drinking and gotten a job he feels that he deserves to be back with his family. This strategy doesn't work. His second strategy comes on the line, 'You know very well what happened.' In this beat, he starts to blame her. The best defence is a good offence. In his third beat, he simply begs her, 'Please you've got to give us another chance.'

- *What are the stakes?* His family and marriage.

- *Character considerations.* We get a hint that Ben might have an anger management problem, when the stage direction tell us that he slams his hand against the wall. The last lines are capitalized, as if he's shouting. Could it be that he is struggling to contain his anger for the whole scene and then he finally explodes?

Scene II

360
Screenplay by Peter Morgan
Directed by Fernando Meirelles
BBC Films

This subtle screenplay, written by Peter Morgan, reads more like play than a film script. That's because it was based on the Arthur Schnitzler classic, *La Ronde*.

Page 36
INT. ROSE'S HOUSE – NIGHT

ROSE is sitting in bed, reading. MICHAEL walks into the room, having put ELLIE to bed . . .

                    MICHAEL
          She went out like a light. She was
          exhausted.

                        ROSE
            She's not the only one.

                        MICHAEL
            I know. It's been a crazy few days.

                        ROSE
            How was Vienna? I haven't asked.

                        MICHAEL
            Fine.

                        ROSE
            Did you get the deal done?

    MICHAEL looks up . . .

                        ROSE
            There was a deal, wasn't there?

                        MICHAEL
            There was. I did.

                        ROSE
            So a trip to Estonia in the near
            future?

                        MICHAEL
                     (clears throat)
            Berlin, actually.

                        ROSE
            Right.
                     (a beat)

                        ROSE
                Never been to Berlin.

    ROSE turns out the light. A silence, then . . .

                        MICHAEL
            And how was everything here? In my
            absence?

ROSE stiffens imperceptibly in the dark . . .

> ROSE
> Fine. I got your message. From last
> night?
>> (a beat)
>
> You sounded emotional.

> MICHAEL
> Did I?

> ROSE
> Something in your voice. Am I wrong?

> MICHAEL
> No. I was.

MICHAEL also stiffens in the dark. He is about
to say something, then stops . . .

> MICHAEL?
> But is it all right if we discuss
> this another time?

> ROSE
>> (relieved)
> Yes, of course.

> MICHAEL
>> (relieved)
> Good night.

> ROSE
> Good night.

They turn in opposite directions, and fall
asleep. At least appear to. But our CAMERA
pulls back to reveal . . .
. . . each is still awake. Their eyes open.
Lost in the private worlds of their own
secrets.

Analysis for Michael

- *Who am I?* Michael Daly, a married businessman, who has just returned from a trip to Vienna. If we read the script, we know the backstory which is that he tried to meet with a prostitute while in Vienna. Some potential buyers discovered this and blackmailed him into making a more expensive deal in Berlin rather than in Estonia.

- *Where am I?* In my bedroom.

- *Who am I talking to?* My wife, Rose.

- *What do I want?* There are different choices an actor can make in this complex scene. It's clear that he feels guilty about his attempted infidelity. One objective is that he wants to confess, but he is afraid of the consequences. Will she leave him? Another objective is that he wants to be intimate with her, to re-connect with her. This delicately written scene is about obstacles and thwarted desires.

- *Where does the scene change?* It changes for him when Rose asks him about Vienna. He's nervous about this. Does she know? In this beat he will try to reassure her. Business is fine. He must also feel a change when she remarks that his voice 'sounded emotional' on the phone. Does she know that he tried to cheat on her? 'Is it alright if we talk about this another time?' he asks, and then they both feel relieved that they can avoid the confrontation. It will be important for the actor to mark each of these subtle beats.

- *What are the stakes?* Their marriage. Will he be able to keep his marriage if he confesses to this betrayal?

- *Technical considerations.* This scene would do best if staged on a bed but we rarely find this in an audition room. Subtle shifts in posture on a chair can indicate the blocking that would take place in the actual staging of the scene.

- *What page are we on?* Page 36. This script is untypical in that it does not follow the Hollywood script formula. The source play, *La Ronde*, has a circular, episodic structure, documenting the relationships of several couples before and after sex. The relationship of this couple (played in the film by Jude Law and Rachel Weisz) opens the film and then we return to them in the end. So in this case we are in the moment before the denouement when the problems resolve.

- *Character considerations.* Michael is an ordinary British family man who is bored with his married life. The story sets him up as a sympathetic character. The actor needs to empathize with him, not judge him.

- *What is the genre?* Drama. The scene reverberates beautifully in its simplicity. Peter Morgan, who writes for stage as well, sets up a Chekhovian style in which more is said in the silences than in the words. Don't throw away the pauses.

Analysis for Rose

- *Who am I?* She is Rose Daly, a married professional woman, who lives in contemporary London.

- *Where am I?* In the bedroom of her London home.

- *Who am I talking to?* Michael Daly, her husband.

- *What do I want?* Rose has just ended an affair with a younger man. Now she is alone with her husband after he has returned from a business trip. She wants to re-connect with him, to renew her romantic relationship with him, to feel intimate with him again. Does she want to confess to him? This is a choice the actor will make.

- *Where does the scene change?* As per the scene analysis for Michael above, the scene has at least three distinct beats. A clear change for her is marked when he asks if they can talk about it later. Thankfully, she doesn't have to confront him now about her indiscretions. Both characters want the same thing but are battling their own obstacles.

- *What are the stakes?* Her marriage and the well-being of their child. Rose, like her husband, is torn about ther infidelity. She wants to be true. This is about a character who is struggling with doing the right thing.

- *Character considerations*. Rachel is a career woman who, like many modern women balances work and family.

Scene III

TV Series: *Crossing Lines*
Screenwriter: Edward Allen Bernero
Producers: Charles Carroll, Moritz
Polter, Rola Bauer
Starring: Donald Sutherland, William
Fichtner
Production Companies: Tandem, NBC,
RTE

225 EXT. REST STOP - NIGHT 225. Pg.
20

Officer BELANGER approaches the Mercedes.
Wilhoit, heart leaping, meets him in the
headlight beams.

> (Wilhoit keeps his gun hidden
> throughout - but we see it enough to
> remind us) -

> BELANGER
Bonsoir, Monsieur.

Wilhoit's voice adopts that syrupy quality as
he smiles wide -

                         WILHOIT
            Bonsoir — though I warn you that is
            close to the limit of my French.

                         BELANGER
                  (English rest of scene)
            American?

                         WILHOIT
                  (nods; offers ID)

               Guilty. With the Diplomatic Corps.
He puts maybe a hint of edge on diplomatic (as
though subtly trying to remind him of
immunity). Belanger looks at the ID, matches
the photo, then looks over Wilhoit to the
Mercedes —

                         WILHOIT
                     (cont'd)
            It's an embassy vehicle.

                         BELANGER
            I see the plates.

Wilhoit tries to remain calm as Belanger's
attention turns back to Wilhoit himself, his
flashlight criss-crossing the American —

                         WILHOIT
            Is there a problem? I had a flat
            fixed and I'm rather in a hurry.

                         BELANGER
            Where'd the blood come from?

                         WILHOIT
            Excuse me?

Belanger points his flashlight at a couple of
blood spots on Wilhoit's shirt —

Oh – that – (laughs) This is funny. I
was turning the bolts and my hand
slipped. I hit myself. My nose bleeds
very easily.

Belanger considers, nods implacably –

> WILHOIT
> (cont'd)
> I don't mean to be disrespectful but
> . . . I really should be getting back
> on the road.

> BELANGER
> I'll help.

> WILHOIT
> No – as I said – it's fixed.

But Belanger pushes past him. He sees
the rim and its condition, with the
ripped fragments of tyre, picks
it up –

> BELANGER
> Open the trunk –

> WILHOIT
> No!

Way louder and more forceful than necessary.
Belanger gauges him. Wilhoit pastes that syrupy
smile on, opens the rear door –

> WILHOIT
> (cont'd)
> I'd rather it go in the back seat.

> BELANGER
> It will tear your leather.

> WILHOIT
> The Ambassador's suitcases and
> personal items are in the trunk. I
> cannot allow them to be damaged. Far

> as the seats go, as I said, it's an
> embassy vehicle – not mine. I'd
> rather damage the seats than the
> Ambassador's boxes. The rich cow
> would sack me within the hour.

Said with just the right amount of class-
distinct derision. Belanger nods
sympathetically, more or less tosses the rim
into the Mercedes' open back seat. Wilhoit
pushes the door closed and thrusts a happy hand
out –

> WILHOIT
> This was so kind of you, Officer.
> Merci. Merci beaucoup.

And Belanger nods, walks back to his car,
Wilhoit, watches (still behind that pasted-on
smile), never moving until the gendarme is
pulling away. As he does, Wilhoit checks his
watch one more time, grabs the jack and stand,
then pops the trunk open.

This scene, from the TV serial *Crossing Lines*, was written by Edward Allen Bernero who pens many popular forensic shows such as *Criminal Minds*. It's a classically formatted scene that typically appears in many different forensic and detective series – the suspect interview. Wilhoit is the special guest role who is in fact the murderer that the police are seeking. Tension ripples this scene, in which the audience knows a dead body festers in the back of Wilhoit's car. We are all hoping, *'Please, Belanger! Make him open the boot!'*

Analysis for Belanger

Belanger is a day player role. It was originally written as 'Gendarme' but was later given a name in order to attract a good actor to the role (an actor is more likely to play a role with a name than a stock character name) and also it's possible that the character will recur in future episodes depending on how the series develops.

Belanger is one of those roles that needs to disappear into the story. A performance that stands out will merely detract from the plot. We need to believe that this is an ordinary day's work for Belanger and that Wilhoit has convinced the gendarme of his legitimacy. The audience's focus will be on Wilhoit. Blending into the story is sometimes difficult for actors to do. Actors are taught to command attention after all, however, in this scene it's about giving stage to the actor playing Wilhoit.

- *Who am I?* A gendarme who is on highway duty tonight.

- *Where am I?* At a rest stop on a highway in France.

- *Who am I talking to?* At first unknown and then he discovers that Wilhoit is an American embassy official in a diplomatic car.

- *What do I want?* To vigilantly investigate on his patrol. He has been alerted that there may be a murder suspect on the road tonight. He needs to confirm that Wilhoit is legitimate and negate the possibility that he is the wanted criminal.

- *What are the stakes?* My job. I could lose my job if a criminal passes through, but my job can also be threatened if there is a complaint against me by the American diplomatic corps.

- *When does the scene change?* The power flips back and forth in this scene. Often it is the policeman who is pulling over the driver who has the power in the scene. But in this case, we are meant to believe that the officer feels outranked by the diplomat and therefore backs down.

- *What page are we on?* Page 20, Scene 225. In this case we have a two-part episode to kick off the season. For a one-hour TV episode, we typically shoot 50-page scripts. Scene 225 means scene 25 of episode two. So we are roughly three-quarters of the way into the story, or halfway through the second episode. This means tensions are rising towards the resolution of the murder mystery.

Analysis for Wilhoit

Gerald Wilhoit is described in the script as a 'short man'. He is one of the monsters with a criminal profile created by former Chicago police officer turned screen-writer Ed Bernero. Through the episodes in this two-part series, the audience comes to know his warped psychological profile. As an off-balance child, his mother tormented him, driving the adult Wilhoit to commit matricide. Now he spends his life re-enacting the crime, while passing as a respectable diplomat. We have to believe that he is in fact diplomatic and this is what has allowed him to pass for so many years. What actor wouldn't want to play this role?

In this case the casting team chose the 5'5" actor Eddie Jemison who has a very pleasant and innocent face. He should look like a normal person.

Typically an actor auditioning for this role will be given at least two scenes in order to demonstrate the character's arch. In this first scene we see the character's everyday, functional mask that he wears to pass in a pedestrian world.

- *Who am I?* Gerald Wilhoit, a diplomat at the American Embassy in Paris. He is also a criminal who has committed matricide and now makes a habit of dressing high-class call girls in his mother's clothes, and performing serial re-enactments of her death.

- *Where am I?* In my diplomat-issued car at a rest stop on a French highway.

- *Who am I talking to?* A gendarme.

- *What do I want?* To convince Belanger that he is innocent so that he can safely bury the body that is in the trunk. His strategies are charm and intimidation.

- *What are the stakes?* Prison. If he is discovered, he will have to stop these re-enactments that are his life-blood.

- *When does the scene change?* There are two crucial moments when Wilhoit is nearly caught out and has to do some fancy footwork. 'Where did the blood come from?' and 'Open the trunk.'

Scene IV

Crossing Lines, second scene

The scene is the second scene for Wilhoit's audition. Usually casters will want to see a lead guest role audition with two separate scenes that demonstrate the arch of the character.

254 EXT. TIERGARTEN PARK - NIGHT 254
Back at the park, Anne-Marie, weak and bleeding, looks back to Wilhoit -

       WILHOIT
   Run.

She is about to when: *FLASH - MEMORY HIT (From Episode One) Anne-Marie and Hickman at the Parc de Saint-Cloud woods -*

      HICKMAN:
   He's a sadist. She was dead the
   moment she showed him fear . . .

BACK TO SCENE
Anne-Marie turns back and looks into Wilhoit's eyes.

       WILHOIT
     (becoming impatient)
   Run.

She gathers strength and straightens, decides to gamble everything on Hickman's theory, defiantly says:

                              ANNE-MARIE
          No.

We HEAR the FAR-OFF SOUND of a CHOPPER but
Wilhoit is completely focused on Anne-Marie –

                              WILHOIT
               What did you say?

Wilhoit is becoming enraged –

          I said 'Run'.

                              ANNE-MARIE
          No.

                              WILHOIT
               I'll kill you right here.

                              ANNE-MARIE
               I'm not afraid of you.

                              WILHOIT
               I'm warning you – you better run –

                              ANNE-MARIE
          No.

His face screws up with rage, not sure what to
do. No one has ever stood up to him this way –

                              WILHOIT
               Run! RUN!
She defiantly stands still. Wilhoit SUDDENLY
PUNCHES HER –

                              WILHOIT
                              (cont'd)
               RUN, YOU BITCH!

Anne-Marie collapses, lays there, looks back up
to him

Wilhoit is reaching that boiling rage we saw in
the Mercedes –

> WILHOIT
> I AM IN CHARGE HERE!

Anne-Marie struggles back to her feet –

*FLASH – MEMORY HIT – SEBASTIAN in the ICC
Headquarters (from Episode One)*

> SEBASTIAN
> He's putting on a show.

> TOMMY
> Tosser like this always is.

BACK TO SCENE

> ANNE-MARIE
> Who am I supposed to be, Gerald?

He is surprised she knows his name.

> Who was it you thought you were
> talking to when you were alone in the
> front seat, Gerald?

> WILHOIT
> YOU BETTER START RUNNING NOW!

FLASH – MEMORY HIT – HICKMAN

> HICKMAN
This guy does the same thing every time, in the
same type of place. He has a ritual that plays
out before the murder.

BACK TO SCENE

> ANNE-MARIE
> Everything is a fantasy. The park,
> the hunting.

FLASH — MEMORY HIT — EVA

> EVA
> He didn't just conceal their
> identities, he erased them.

BACK TO SCENE

> ANNE-MARIE
> You dressed me — who am I? Who do you
> think I am?

> WILHOIT
> RUN!!!!!

> ANNE-MARIE
> NO!

Wilhoit takes only a moment before losing it
altogether —

> WILHOIT
> YOU BITCH! YOU DO WHAT I SAY. YOU DO
> IT NOW! YOU DO WHAT I SAY!

Instead of that she whips on him with equally
venomous anger —

*FLASH — MEMORY HIT — SIENNA Looking over the
show in the park (from Episode One) —*

> SIENNA
> There's . . . it's odd — it's
> actually a very old style.

BACK TO SCENE

> ANNE-MARIE
> Is it your mother?

Which actually seems to get through to him —

ANNE-MARIE
(cont'd)

The older dress, the older shoes. I
am not your mother. I'm a detective
in the French National Police. You
have taken a police officer –

Then, on the breeze, VOICES seemingly from
every direction:

VARIOUS VOICES (O.S.)
Anne-Marie!

Wilhoit looks around, confused, then back at
her –

ANNE-MARIE
They know who you are.

WILHOIT
Who . . .

ANNE-MARIE
The police. I'm Detective Lansing.
You're sick and I can get you –

And the air CRASHES out of her as Wilhoit
SAVAGELY STRIKES her in the gut. She goes down
hard and we can't tell if he stabbed her or
punched her, but she is hurt.

WILHOIT
I am not sick, you filthy bitch!

She writhes there on the ground. Wilhoit stands
above her, eyes darting around him. The VOICES
are getting LOUDER and CLOSER. He covers his
ears then RUNS OFF into the woods.

Second scene analysis for Wilhoit

This denouement scene allows the actor auditioning for Wilhoit to expose the darkest side of this character. It's an excellent contrast to the scene with the police officer in which he presents his diplomatic face and we see him passing as a normal person.

- *What do I want?* In this scene Wilhoit wants to act out his fantasy. He thrives on the thrill and power of seeing women run in fear of him. The adult Wilhoit reverts into the state of a powerless child who was manipulated by his mother.

- *Who am I talking to?* A female victim, whom he is imagining is his mother so he can re-enact her murder.

- *What are the stakes?* Life and death. Wilhoit cannot live without these re-enactments. The actor needs to make choices of extreme urgency to make this scene work. The challenge for the actor is how to make this demented character believable. Most of us (fortunately) don't wish to live out these types of deranged fantasies. So the actor auditioning for this role will have to exercise his imagination in the extreme sense, pushing the boundaries of human behaviour. In this character's mind, his actions are deserved and necessary.

- *Where does the scene change?* It changes when he realizes Anne-Marie won't be like his other victims. She won't play by the rules. This makes him progressively angry.

Analysis for Anne-Marie

Anne-Marie is a series regular, a member of the international police team who busts crime across international borders.

- *Who am I?* Anne-Marie San, French police officer and member of the ICC (International Criminal Court) anti-crime team.

- *Where am I?* A sting operation has led her to the Tiergarten Park in Berlin, Germany. She's been captured by the main target of her criminal investigation.

- *Who am I talking to?* Gerald Wilhoit, who her team has suspected in the murder of several women whose bodies have been discovered in parks across Europe.

- *What do I want?* She is fighting for her life. She does this by recalling what her team has been discovering about him (in the flashbacks), and targeting it against him. He has weakened her so she doesn't have her normal strength to fight him physically. She must use a psychological approach.

- *Where are the changes?* The scene changes when she recalls what her colleagues have said about his psychological profile and makes the choice to break his script. If she refuses to submit, he won't know what to do and this is her best chance for survival.

- *What are the stakes?* Life and death.

Bibliography

Biskind, Peter (1998) *Easy Riders, Raging Bulls: How the Sex 'n' Drugs 'n' Rock 'n' Roll Generation Saved Hollywood.* Bloomsbury, London

Caine, Michael (1997) *Acting in Film: An Actor's Take on Movie Making.* Applause Books, New York

Chekhov, Michael (1953) *To the Actor on the Technique of Acting.* Harper and Row, New York

Gillespie, Bonnie (2009) *Self-Management for Actors: Getting Down to (Show) Business.* Cricket Feet Publishing, Los Angeles

Hirshenson, Janet and Jenkins, Jane with Kranz, Rachel (2006) *A Star is Found: Our Adventures Casting Some of Hollywood's Biggest Movies.* Harcourt, Inc., San Diego

Hyde, Lewis (2007) *The Gift: Creativity and the Artist in the Modern World.* Vintage Books USA, Random House, New York

Levitin, Daniel (2006) *This is Your Brain on Music: The Science of a Human Obsession.* Penguin Group, Harmondsworth

Mamet, David (1999) *True and False: Heresy and Common Sense for the Actor.* Vintage Books, USA, Random House, New York

Merlin, Joanna (2001) *Auditioning: An Actor-Friendly Guide.* Vintage Books USA, Random House, New York

Murch, Walter (2001) *In the Blink of an Eye.* Silman-James Press, Los Angeles

Shurtleff, Michael (1978) *Audition: Everything an Actor Needs to Know to Get the Part.* Walker and Company, New York

Stanislavski, Constantine (1948) *Creating a Role.* Translated by Elizabeth Reynolds Hapgood. Routledge, London

Tucker, Patrick (2003) *Secrets of Screen Acting.* Theatre Arts Books, Routledge, London

Weston, Judith (1996) *Directing Actors: Creating Memorable Performances for Film and Television.* Michael Wiese Productions, Los Angeles

Index

INDEX